SCREENWRITING

STEP-BY-STEP

3 Manuscripts in 1 Book, Including: How to Write a Screenplay, Story Structure and Character Development

Sandy Marsh

More by Sandy Marsh

Discover all books from the Writing Best Seller Series by Sandy Marsh at:

bit.ly/sandy-marsh

Book 1: *How to Write a Novel*

Book 2: *Outlining*

Book 3: *Story Structure*

Book 4: *Plotting*

Book 5: *Character Development*

Book 6: *How to Write a Screenplay*

Themed book bundles available at discounted prices:

bit.ly/sandy-marsh

Table of Contents

HOW TO WRITE A SCREENPLAY

STEP-BY-STEP

ESSENTIAL SCREENPLAY FORMAT, SCRIPTWRITER AND MODERN SCREENPLAY WRITING TRICKS ANY WRITER CAN LEARN

SANDY MARSH

BOOK 1: HOW TO WRITE A SCREENPLAY

STEP-BY-STEP

Essential Screenplay Format, Scriptwriter and Modern Screenplay Writing Tricks Any Writer Can Learn

Sandy Marsh

reparation, damages, or monetary loss due to the information herein, either directly or indirectly.

Respective authors own all copyrights not held by the publisher.

The information herein is offered for informational purposes solely and is universal as so. The presentation of the information is without a contract or any type of guarantee assurance.

The trademarks that are used are without any consent, and the publication of the trademark is without permission or backing by the trademark owner. All trademarks and brands within this book are for clarifying purposes only and are the owned by the owners themselves, not affiliated with this document.

Table of Contents

Introduction

I want to thank you and congratulate you for purchasing the book *"How to Write a Screenplay: Step-by-Step | Essential Screenplay Format, Scriptwriter and Modern Screenplay Writing Tricks Any Writer Can Learn"*.

In this book, you will find all of the information you need to begin writing a screenplay, the details on the specifics of the most common types of screenplays, tips on creating believable characters in your screenplays, how to create a first draft and get to work on editing and tips that have worked for the experts.

You will need the information in this book if you want to create a successful script that will catch the eye of producers to get it to the big screen.

To not develop your ability to write a properly formatted screenplay would be Hollywood murder to your career. Style is everything, and this book covers that.

It's time for you to create an amazing screenplay.

Chapter 1: What is a Screenplay?

A screenplay (also known as a script) is a written output made for a television show, a movie, a video, or a game. When it is written for television, it is also called as teleplay.

Screenplay consists of action and dialogue. Action is where a character is noted to do an action, and a dialogue is where the character is speaking. These two components make up around ninety percent of a screenplay.

What sets a screenplay apart from a stageplay are the use of sluglines. This designates where the scene takes place, and what time of day it is, along with the weather that is occurring at the time. These descriptions are important so that the director can make sure that the scenes are set up properly.

Physical format

Screenplays are printed very specifically. They are also all put together specifically as well. This makes it easier for a producer to get through a bunch at one time. They are generally bound with a cardboard cover and a back page to protect the script when it is handled. Oftentimes, the first copy of the script is the only copy. While it is backed up, it takes a lot of paper to print a script most times, so it is important to save where you can.

In America, the script is usually printed single-spaced on letter size paper. It is printed using 12 point courier font. When it is bound, it is bound using a three-hole punch and held together with two brads. One at the top and one at the bottom. This makes it easier to flip through the script quickly.

Reading copies, those which are distributed, are often printed double-sided to reduce paper waste. This is because there are often more copies that will need to be printed later on, and scripts already take so much paper to print anyway, that finding ways to cut down is a must.

Scripts can often be delivered electronically, but many companies require that a certain amount of copies be handed to the company, or at least mailed if travel is not possible.

Screenplay formats

Screenplays come with a certain set of standards that must be met. These standards are ones that help keep everything uniform and allow for easy reading. They form a sort of blueprint for movies and other screenplays. This also allows a company to distinguish those who take things seriously, from those who have a more laissez-faire attitude. There are software packages out there that can help assist with the formatting of screenplays. This makes it easier to ensure that you will have a professional looking piece to show prospective producers. SmartKey, the first screenwriting software, sent codes to existing word processors. However, the ones today have their own macro entities.

Feature film

If you intend to get a motion picture on the big screen, there are a lot of stipulations for how you have to write your screenplay. The headings, formatting, and spacing all have to meet a specific set of guidelines. While the guidelines may vary from country to country, they are all pretty similar in the fact that they have to be uniform. This is because the rate of transfer from page to screen remains around one minute. This gives a rough estimate of how long the piece will run when taken to the big screen. However, some things often get cut, so it is a very rough estimate.

Nevertheless, if you ever want anybody to not only read what you have written, but to truly take it seriously, you will need to stick to the rules in order to ensure that they have as few obstacles between them and getting to the heart of your story. In general, you can think of the concept of screenplay formatting as mainly an aesthetic choice to ensure that every page of your screenplay is as clear and legible as possible. Each script you turn in should always be written in 12-point, Courier font. This goes for movies or television.

The Slug: Luckily, the Hollywood script format is simple once you learn the basics. Every screenplay is divided into different scenes, each of which represents a different location that the story is viewed from. When a new location is introduced in a screenplay, it needs to be described in a specific way so that the person reading it can automatically picture three key pieces of information. They will need to know whether the scene is taking place inside or outside, the time of day it is and the actual location. Together, these three things form what is known as the slug.

Each scene introduction is going to be written so that it appears on a single line, which will include the location details as well as relevant information about the time of day. The majority of slugs will start with either EXT. or INT., meaning exterior or interior respectively. In general, a slug with start with EXT. or INT. and end with either NIGHT OR DAY unless the specific time of day is crucial to the scene. The only time this will not be the case is during parts of the script where the action is repeatedly cutting between two places or is moving through a number of locations, following a character who starts out from a location that has already been defined. For example: EXT. CAVE – DAY

If you have already introduced the cave in the previous example, then you could simplify by writing BACK TO CAVE.

If a character is moving throughout multiple locations inside a predefined location, such as a house, you can write the intervening slugs as KITCHEN or BEDROOM to maintain the flow of the story while still providing the reader with the details they need.

While not required, the slug often also includes the indicator SUPER which is followed by identifying information and indicates what would be superimposed on the screen for example SUPER: 10 years earlier.

If you are writing a conversation between two individuals who are not speaking to one another directly, you can use the indicator INTERCUT BETWEEN after both of the settings have been determined with a standard slug.

The shot: While the shot will also appear in capital letters with a similar type of formatting, it serves a different function when compared to a slug and shot not be confused with it.

As an example: ANGLE ON JACK, C.U. ON GUN. When writing your screenplay, you will use this technique to draw specific attention to an element of the action. It is typically followed by its own description, almost written as an aside, that is always ended with the indicator BACK TO SCENE before the action from the main scene resumes.

Action elements: An action element is going to come directly after the slug and is preceded by a blank line that runs the length of the page. The action element is responsible for setting the scene, literally, as it describes the setting. In it you will introduce what your characters are doing in the scene that will ideally naturally set the scene for what is going to come next. Any action written in this section should be written in real time, which means you are going to want to write as crisply and cleanly as possible in an effort to convey exactly what the audience will see on screen.

When you write your action elements, it is important to leave out as many extraneous details as possible as this makes the script easier to shoot as fewer unique props will be required. The only time you are going to want to go over the top with atmospheric descriptions is when the atmosphere is crucial to what is taking place on screen. For example, if you picture your favorite horror movie, you can bet that the scene that introduced the main location contain an action element with descriptive text.

However, if you are writing scenes that include lots of tense, back and forth dialogue, or action, then you are going to want to do your best to ensure descriptions are kept to an overall minimum. This will help to create an overall feeling of watching the scene play out in real time which naturally makes your script feel as though it could easily be adapted to the big screen.

In order to write action that plays on the page, the easiest thing to do is picture yourself having coffee with a friend and discussing something interesting you saw on your way to the café. This way you will be sure that you cut out all the filler and only focus on the parts that really matter. During these scenes, you are going to want to keep your paragraphs short, no more than five lines in a paragraph, no matter what. Be sure to capitalize any sound effects that are used. Between each paragraph you are going to want to leave two blank lines. By splitting up your descriptions and your action, you are adding an overall visual emphasis to your story, making it feel more like a movie throughout.

When introducing characters, capitalize the entire name, you are also going to want to include a specific gender as well as age. This information is not only going to be crucial when it comes to understanding what is going on in the story, but when it comes to things like budgeting and casting as well. Make sure you don't go so far as to describe specific hairstyles and clothing, except in situations where it is crucial to the plot. You are also going to want to avoid using parenthesis to indicate action when introducing a character. This means no: BOB (cracks a beer).

When describing movement, you are going to never want to use the word camera. Instead, replace it with the word we. This means no: the camera follows, instead it would be: we follow…

Setting up dialogue: The name of the character who is speaking is going to appear in all caps, tabbed in to almost the center of the page and then directly followed by relevant dialogue. The name of the person speaking can either be the name of the character (BOB) or a description if the person isn't known (MAN IN BLACK). Occupations are also acceptable if they are easily identifiable by the average person. If a character is going to play more than an incidental role in the story they should have a name. Be consistent when you refer to a named character, this means no calling BOB by his name in once scene and then by his last name in the next.

Writing Dialogue: The dialogue itself is going to appear located between the left margin, which is where the slug and the action are written and the margin where the character name is written. Writing good dialogue is certainly an art form all to itself, and most new screenwriters make the mistake of over-writing their dialogue.

The end result of this, in most cases is going to be dialogue that comes off more like a play than a movie, which tends to make scenes seem slower than they might otherwise be. It is important to try and keep your dialogue informal, while at the same time not stuffing it full of as much slang as you can manage. If it is important to the story that you character have a regional dialect, you can mention it when you describe them initially, but do not write out their lines in a regional dialect, unless it is a single line written in such a way to indicate emphasis.

When writing dialogue, it is important to make an effort to reflect the personality of each character in the things that they say, while also walking a fine line of not overdoing it. This will make it easier for the reader to picture the conversation as if it were actually happening, as opposed to two characters in a book, spouting soliloquies at one another. This also relates to the way in which key information is relied by the characters in the scenes. You should aim to express inner feelings in a subtle manner, without resorting to on the nose writing where each character simply says what they are thinking or feeling. Your overall goal should be to make the reader, and thus ultimately the audience, feel as though they are a fly on the wall for a real conversation.

Keep in mind that during almost all conversations, the primary players are rarely going to come right out and say whatever it is they mean. Instead, the conversation is going to have subtext. This means you are going to want to leave out bits and pieces of what exactly is going on and allow the audience the opportunity to figure it out on their own. Not only will this make the scene feel more natural, it will be more interesting to watch (or read) as well. For example, in the movie Jerry Maguire, the character of Jerry Maguire uses the phrase "You complete me" to indicate that he is finally ready to express his feelings for the romantic lead. In this instance, the audience knows he means he loves her because earlier in the movie there was a scene of a deaf couple using sign language and a discussion of the sign for love.

While this example is just a little thing, it still makes the audience think, which is a key to keeping them interested in what is taking place in front of them. As such, you are going to want to consider every line of dialogue that you write and the other possible ways that the same intent could be expressed without directly coming right out and saying it.

Parenthetical information: Any parenthetical information that you need to include in your script is going to appear left indented within brackets, underneath the character name. They are used only to express the emotion the character is currently feeling in the moment. For example, (laughing), (angry), or (upset). Any parenthetical information you provide should always be short, descriptive and to the point. As with any ancillary information, they should only be used when they are crucial to the plot.

Transition elements: Certain transitions are going to be optional, these include things like DISSOLVE TO: or CUT TO:. When you use them, they are going to need to be right indented, not flush right, and should only come after a blank line on the page and should always be followed by two blank lines as well. When you come to the end of page without completing a scene, the scene transition should always stay with the shot that was just completed which means you will never start a new page with either DISSOLVE TO: or CUT TO:, those would remain at the bottom of the previous page.

Transitions are primarily used to denote a major shift in time or location, and sometimes, like using MATCH CUT TO:, for effect. You are generally going to want to leave out transition any time you find yourself rapidly cutting between scenes when adding them in will noticeably disrupt the flow of the sequence in question. This is particularly true for chase or montage scenes.

Chapter 2: Television Screenwriting Considerations

The format for television shows differs depending on how long they are supposed to run. Hour-long dramas are written up much like a movie screenplay, however, there are always breaks for act changes. Meanwhile, sitcoms and other, shorter, television shows are written a little differently which means their scripts have different formats to discern what they are supposed to be. The biggest difference between television and movie screenplays is that the level of standardization between genres, or even varying shows is far less well-defined. There are still going to have some hard and fast rules, however, which means the first thing you are going to want to do before you write a spec script is to read several scripts for the show you are going to be writing for so that you get a feel for what makes it unique.

Nevertheless, there are going to be some similarities in this field as well, and it is important that you understand what they are to ensure you get off on the right foot. One thing that is never going to change is the structure of the show in question. A 30-

minute television show is 22 minutes of content and 8 minutes of advertising (in general) and an hourlong show is typically 45 minutes of content and 15 minutes of commercials. The breaks need to be located in the right spots, which means the act breaks, with two or three additional breaks, depending on the network, for hourlong shows.

Drama

When it comes to writing drama, a good rule of thumb is to start every scene already in progress and make sure to move on to the next too early as opposed to too late. Additionally, you are going to want to be extremely selective when it comes to the scenes you do include, each one will need to either develop your characters or advance your plot, there is little room for anything else. The scenes that are going to end on commercial breaks should end on points of high dramatic tension, even if it is not integral to the plot as a whole. Above all you are going to want to keep your focus on showing, rather than telling.

Common types of dramas: There are several major types of dramas that tend to get produced, this is not to say that nothing else is ever going to get on the air, they are just the evergreen types of shows you can always expect to find somewhere on the dial. The first is the procedural, while this was once largely classified to police shows, there are now countless variations on the traditional solve a mystery in an hour formula, and you can find everything from medical to supernatural procedurals on television these days. The next type is the workplace drama, where there is equal focus on the jobs the characters do as well as on their personal lives.

After the success of *Game of Thrones*, the genre drama went from a small niche to big business. These types of shows typically blend fantasy or science fiction with more grounded characters and interpersonal stories. Finally, there are dramas found on premium cable channels, which can fall into any of the categories, but typically deal in much more extreme content matter and also don't need to worry about the traditional act breaks found in non-premium scripts.

Formatting: When it comes to formatting an hourlong script, if you don't have any sample material to look at, you can safely assume that it will be formatted in the same way a feature script would be, more or less, with the biggest difference being the act breaks. Don't forget, the average page of script is assumed to be about one minute, and the average script tends to come in at no more than 60 pages.

The first page, the cover page, that you provide should include the name of the show above the title of the episode above the writer's name. The next page will be the title name and it should include the same information as the cover page as well as your contact information printed below it.

The average episode is broken up into a teaser, which sets the stage for the episode and is what the viewer will see before the title sequence. The rest of the script will then be broken into four acts. Again, this is only an estimate as there are numerous shows that alter this format in one way or another, the best choice is always going to be tracking down a sample script from the show in question if you hope to be taken seriously.

Each act is going to be given a numerical designation and center at the top of the page that starts the act. Broadly speaking, both Act One and Act 1 are acceptable, just ensure that you are consistent throughout. Likewise, the end of each act should by bookended by End Act _. This should be two lines below the final line of text from the act, bolded and centered. FADE or CUT may be used to end a scene, but this is not required. A simple scene slug will do instead. Each new act should then start fresh at the top of a new page.

The average page breakdown per section works out as follows

Teaser: Between two and four pages

Act one: Between 14 and 15 pages

Act two: Between 14 and 15 pages

Act three: Between 14 and 15 pages

Act four: Between 14 and 15 pages

Tag: Between one and two pages

Total: Between 59 and 66 pages

Narrative structure: Broadly speaking, you are going to want to follow a standard three act structure for your script, the first act should set up the goal for the episode and the end of the first act will generally end with them failing to reach some sort of instant gratification. The second act will further complicate whatever it is that the main character is trying to do, while simultaneously raising the stakes. The end of this act will find the character at their lowest point for the entire episode.

Act three typically begins with something that renews the character's resolve and pushes them to get right to the point where they are going to attempt to overcome their obstacle. Finally, act four resolves everything, though the amount to which this is the case is going to be determined by whether or not the episodes are designed for standalone or serialized viewing.

As a general rule, you can expect the average modern series to include the main plot as well as two subplots that all take place at the same time. The main story is the A plot, the B plot is then the more involved of the two subplots while the C plot, also known as the runner, is typically limited to character building moments. These typically occur about three times throughout the episode. If your subplots are going to be referencing specific details from other plotlines of the television show in question, you will need to indicate where in the series continuity it takes place on the title page.

Sitcoms

The first thing you need to understand about writing situation comedies, is that you already need to be adept at telling jokes in order to succeed in the medium. Specifically, you need to concern yourself with timing as if a joke is executed poorly, especially on the page without a comedic actor to save it, it will fall flat every time.

Multicamera: When considering writing a sitcom script, the first thing you will need to consider is if the show you are considering writing a script for is filmed in the multicamera or single camera mindset. In general, you can expect a multicamera shows to have two acts while single camera shows will more often have three.

The general format for a multicamera show is as follows:

FADE IN: this should always be written in capital letters and underlined.

SCENE the scene should be numbered, capitalized and underlined with two spaces above and below it.

Slug the slug should always be underlined .

(Character list) the character list should be written directly underneath the slug and is used to tell the reader which characters are going to be in the scene. It should be encapsulated inside a parenthesis.

DESCRIPTIONS AND ACTIONS both required actions and relevant descriptions are always capitalized, don't forget to keep these to only plot specific requirements.

CHARACTER INTROS this should always be written in capital letters and underlined.

CAMERA INSTRUCTIONS, SPECIAL EFFFECTS AND SOUND EFFECTS this should always be written in capital letters and underlined.

CHARACTER NAMES AND DIALOUGE these should always be written in capital letters and double spaced.

(PERSONAL DIRECTION) this will appear within lines of dialogue, in all capital letters and enclosed in a parenthesis.

The first page after the cover and title page of average sitcom script will start with the name of the show written in capital letters, exactly six lines down from the top of the page and surrounded by quotation marks. Six lines below this you will want to center ACT ONE followed by A on the next line, which indicates the scene, also centered. 8 lines underneath this you will then write FADE IN: so that it aligns with a 1.4-inch margin. This should be followed by the list of characters that is going to appear in the scene. Each page should be numbered and also include the letter corresponding to the scene in question.

The second scene, and each additional scene will then start on a new page. 21 lines down from the top of the page you will put the scene designation, centered. Six lines below that you will then write the slug. Each act will also begin on a new page. When you are writing dialogue, you are going to want to make it double spaced to ensure it is easy to read. When you write stage direction, ensure you do so in all capital letters in order to more easily distinguish them from the dialogue. Each page should contain plenty of white space to ensure actors have space to write their own notes. In general, the following page breakdown should apply.

Teaser: Between one and two pages

Act one: Between 13 and 20 pages, depending on if the story has two or three acts

Act two: Between 13 and 20 pages, depending on if the story has two or three acts

Act three: Between 0 and 13 pages, depending on if the story has two or three acts

Tag: Between one and three pages

Total: Between 40 and 48 pages

Single camera: Single camera shows are typically going to be formatted more like dramas, though again, specific shows may vary. Even if they have commercial breaks, they may not have a traditional three act structure, especially if the entire season is serialized. When writing dialogue, as well as stage direction, you are going to want to make sure that both are single-spaced. Additionally, each character should have their name written in all capital letters the first time they are introduced onscreen. These scripts are typically the tightest of the three, rarely coming in at more than 32 pages in length.

Additional Tips to Keep In Mind

When writing for a sitcom, above all else you need to nail the tone as well as the voice of each character on the show you are writing a script for. The people who will be reading spec scripts know their shows inside and out and they will respond better to those they can tell know it just as well.

Your spec script should be thought of as your portfolio, resume and calling card all in one. As such, you better make sure it is great if you ever hope to get your foot in the door. In addition to being a tight, well-written story, your script needs to be completely free of all errors, if grammar isn't your strong suit, get someone else to edit your script for you. A lack of concern over the little things won't reflect well overall and could easily be the deciding factor between you and another aspiring screenwriter.

In general, you are going to want to stay away from writing a pilot before you have even landed a job in the industry as pilots from unknowns are rarely picked up. With that being said, however, if you have a great idea for a show, write the pilot episode and then write two or three more. By this point your characters will be more well-established and you can show the reader what your average episode is going to be like. This is crucial as the early episodes of many shows are spent establishing character relationships and interactions, leaving less time for traditional activities and jokes and leading to scripts that seem limp.

Avoid using parentheticals whenever possible. Only leave them in if they clearly enhance the dialogue in a specific way. One of the only acceptable times is when the parenthetical will explain body language that will indicate that the character is saying one thing while clearly meaning something else. Likewise, you are going to want to avoid unnecessary explanations, if you can't make the scene work without explaining it, you should cut it, period. Finally, avoid adding scenes just to fill space, if you can fill out a full-length script with useful content it's time to go back to the drawing board.

Chapter 3: How to Create Characters

When it comes to writing a compelling screenplay, the first thing you that is likely going to come to you is going to be the basic outline of the plot. In order to ensure that this basic idea matures organically into a fully fleshed-out screenplay, the first thing you are going to want to do is more fully consider the characters that are going to be going with you on the adventure you are creating. You will find that getting to know your characters more intimately will make the process of actually connecting the dots on the story much more manageable.

You are not just going to want to only focus on creating a protagonist, you are going to want to consider who are going to be the main characters of your story, both protagonists and antagonists, and write character biographies as well. In fact, this is encouraged, especially if you are writing a feature length screenplay. You want a solid backstory and a solid foundation for writing your character into your story. This is a great way to create a very strong character that will draw the audience's attention until the very end.

Always remember the Theory of Illumination. This theory states that every character reflects on your main character. Their relationships, and their development, eventually lead them to your main character. While giving every character a fully-developed backstory on screen is not recommended, knowing the details of a character's life will make them easier to write for in addition to making them seem more well-rounded as a whole.

This means that you aren't going to want to flesh out all of your character bios in a single evening, you need to spend some time to really think each of your characters through. Take a few days where you spend a few hours to think about your characters, this time should be spent without distractions. No phones, no TV, no music, just you and your thoughts, because you want your character to be authentic, not a copy of a distraction that sticks in your mind. You want a truly original person, not a second-rate copy of someone else's character.

Then, you just start writing. Write anything that you feel is relevant to your character's development. Just let your character grow, and pretty much create themselves, with only the manipulation of the outline you have decided on. This is called free association. Free associating is where you let the words take you wherever, and you merely go along for the ride. This allows you to ensure that your character is not too stiff. You want your character to be real, not forced.

This is not say that everything you write during this period is going to be usable, and indeed much of it may be garbage. However, if you can successfully manage to channel your character for this process you never know what useful information you may end up discovering.

You want to follow every major aspect of your character, true, but you cannot neglect the small things that add up to make your character truly who they are. Remember, people are not made up of only the defining moments in their lives, they are also made up of all of the little, seemingly insignificant moments inbetween. You could possibly do a portion where you outline what their day looks like from the time they wake up, to the time they go to sleep. This will help you better establish the type of person your character will be as well.

If you find an area in your character's life, and you are not sure exactly which way to proceed, let the cards fall where they may. If you are still unsure, do a little research, and go from there. You want to know everything about your character, but you can also be surprised where the words take you. Remember, if you don't like what you come up with you can always scrap it later. When writing your script you should only be focused on creating the best story possible, not with how long the process takes you.

Write! Do not worry about if other people will love it, because if you do not, then no one will. You have to first and foremost be able to stand behind your screenplay one hundred percent. Otherwise, it will not be taken seriously. As the quality of your overall screenplay is going to be dependent on the strength of your characters, it equally stands to reason that you need to love them first, before you worry about anything else.

It is important to create dynamic characters and to keep yourself in line with how you want your screenplay to go. The character has to fall in line with what you want to achieve, and yet they also have to bring a certain element to the table as well. They have to create a little bit of chaos, while also maintaining the peace so to speak.

Imagine you are walking a tightrope. You have to have precision balance. That is what making a character is like. You have to have some flaws as no one wants to root for a character that is perfect. However, too many flaws will make your character seem like a mess, and unless your character is actually a mess, you want them to be relatable. So, you have to walk that tightrope between peace and chaos. This is harder than most people think. As it becomes too easy to make a character extremely flawed, or completely perfect. It becomes too easy to fall to one side or the other, and you have to stay in the middle. It is okay to teeter a few times, but you have to pull your balance back up and continue on.

If you are not able to do so, you will find that the whole story veers out of control, and that can make your screenplay less than desirable. This is what you want to avoid for a plethora of reasons, but the first being that you

Here are my top 5 tips for writing stronger characters into your screenplay:

Make your character likable early on: You have to make your character someone that the audience wants to spend at least ninety minutes with. This means you have to make them likable from the get-go. Even if you think the character is interesting, if they are not very positive, or they are annoying, the audience will lose interest before you get to the good parts of the character.

You want the audience to be able to identify with the character because that is what draws their interest in. The main character should be written as the protagonist, this way the main person is not a self-serving, negative drawback to the screenplay, unless the entire purpose of the screenplay is to chronicle their downfall or their redemption. In general, however, people want to see the negative characters portrayed as the antagonist. This way there is some balance between good and bad though, typically, good will win out in the end.

Your character does not have to be perfect, they just have to have some redeeming qualities. These qualities will help your character reach out to the audience in a way that keeps them interested. You can do this by making the dialogue witty and conversational. You can make them do a kind act in the beginning, such as saving a cat from a tree. In fact, there is an entire screenwriting book, entitled *Save the Cat* for just that reason. Regardless of the setup you choose, you just have to make sure that you set the tone for a likable character early on in the story. This is important, because if you do not, you may find that you lose your audience's interest before even grabbing a hold of it properly.

If you have a character that maybe does not have the best qualities, then it is important to include other, worse, characters to make him seem better in comparison. For example, if you have a character that may be in prison, you want to make him better than the other prisoners. Your character does not have to be a saint, just better than the others, and more relatable than a villain. They have to have a sense of purpose about them, to attract the audience to the plot line, and help them retain their interest until the very end. A complex character cannot get lost in his flaws.

Build realistic & detailed characters: While the character is who your person is, characterization is what they are. One is the true deep soul of the character, the other is the shallower, facade that they present to the rest of the world. For example, you could have a lonely woman who just wants someone to love as a character, but her characterization could be a CEO of a company who acts like she does not need anything from anyone. This is characterization. Sometimes the two are similar, and sometimes they are polar opposites. Like a hard, edgy teen is truly a softy on the inside. These contrasts, when revealed, make for a more detailed, believable characters, and a better storyline. People love to be surprised and love finding out more about the characters in a story. So, you have to make sure that you detail their characterization precisely. You want to make sure that you put

some emphasis on who they are, but also what they are as well –
the inside and the outside.

Writing strong characterization is important on so many
levels. First off, a realistically depicted character will add a lot of
realism to your piece. I cannot count how many times I've seen
the same generic antagonist in a film that had zero original
characterization, which ultimately completely diminished their
importance in the film. But even outside of just adding realism to
the characters, it can also help you as a writer to tell your story
more intuitively and dramatically.

Just like you want to write a character biography, you also
want to create characterization sheets. These help you discern
what your character will be like throughout most of the
screenplay. You can do this quickly, through another round of
free association. Give your character choices, as if they were
living, breathing, individuals. It is important for you to be free
flowing with your characters so that they feel authentic and
realistic. If you try to force your character to completely match
someone who inspires you, the character will feel forced. Let the
character speak to you. Which, coincidentally, brings us directly
up to the next tip.

Let your character make the decisions for you: Many writers feel that their screenplay has to be completely mapped out before they even begin writing, and while it is important for you to make sure that you have the structure outlined, it is equally important to let your characters breathe, otherwise the setting will feel fake and forced, which is the opposite of what you want.

Rather than forcing your character into a box that you have neatly outlined before you have even touched the first sentence, you should let your character make their own decisions. This may sound silly because you are the writer, but the truth is, once you have spent enough time with your characters this will seem much more reasonable. Once you have spent enough time chronicling their likes and dislikes, you will find that you will be able to easily picture what they would do when confronted with a specific decision. You want them to come alive and come off the page, which means you have to let the characters take control sometimes. This allows the scene to feel more realistic, and give it more depth.

While your character may be an extension of yourself, they are also a separate entity from you as well and should be treated as such. With that being said, however, if you give a character a trait that you share with them, then it becomes much easier to anticipate how they would act in a given situation as you can use your own experiences as a point of reference.

If you have already created a character biography and a characterization sheet, then this should be an easy thing to do. You should know your character inside out, and as your character grows, how they will make their way through the story should become clear. So, while you might have thought the character could go one way, you may be surprised when you get to that point, and find that another solution suddenly makes more sense.

Likewise, you are going to want your characters to grow organically which means letting them change as the story dictates, as opposed to forcing them to remain in a predetermined box. Not only will this do a disservice to the character overall, it is unsatisfying for an audience to leave a character exactly where they started, either mentally, emotionally or physically, unless that fact is central to the overall plot. You want them to be like real people, because they will be portrayed by real people, and your target audience will be real people, so you have to make sure that your character has depth.

Approach the early drafts with an open mind, and that will help you build an organic, relatable character. Even if it means you have to change a lot because one choice changes everything.

You will find that the more you let your character choose, the more realistic the story will feel, and the more interest the story will garner. This is what you are looking for because you want the character to draw the audience in. It is important that you write some serious choices in as well, as a screenplay without real consequences is likely lacking in dramatic tension as well.

Give your character compelling dialogue: Dialogue was touched on earlier, but it is important enough to warrant further consideration. All of your characters need to have a strong dialogue. This will establish who they are within their first few lines. Even if they do not have a lot of lines, the ones that they have should be solid, and discerning.

So much can be conveyed by the simple use of dialogue. Accent can determine where the character is from. Their sentence structure can determine how educated they are. The tone of voice can determine if they are introverted or extroverted. All of this and more can be shown just by how the character's lines are written.

Something as simple as a scene where a character is running errands, and talking to the people they meet can tell a lot about the character. This may seem odd, but it is true because they are showing a piece of themselves in their everyday life.

Even though the narrative films are fiction, people want them to seem as realistic as they possibly can. This is because people like what they can relate to. They want to be able to feel a connection to a character, even if it is an animated character. Dialogue is a great way to do that.

Compelling dialogue is not always a lot of dialogue. You could have a character that speaks very little, and yet they could be a very dynamic character. How you set up their dialogue really sets the tone for how they are portrayed. You have to make sure that no matter how many lines of dialogue a character has, they are set up to portray a depth to that character.

Something that you want to stay away from is one-dimensional dialogue. This is where all of your characters speak the same. Even if they are all from the same area and same family, every person speaks differently. While similar characters may have similar dialogue, they should also have their own unique characteristics in their dialogue. This will help you discern the different people when the storyline starts speeding up. If you have all the same dialogue, the characters will blend into one another.

#5 – Think like an actor and give your character a point of view

One of the most important things to think about is the character's point of view. As the writer, you see everything, but the main character does not. You have to make sure that you are writing with the character's point of view to ensure that confusion does not set in by the character knowing something that would be impossible for them to know. This clutters things up and makes it hard to keep the scenes straight.

If you are laughing at this tip, you need it the most. You cannot just slap a character down all willy-nilly, you have to put some thought into it. You want a character that will be easy to figure out so that the actor can do the character the justice they deserve.

The most important reason to write a strong point of view is that it gives a line for the story to follow. The audience needs to understand where the character stands, and if the character does not have a solid point of view, then this gets harder to do, and it gets frustrating for the audience, the actors, and everyone involved in the creation of the work you have worked so hard on.

Have you ever seen *Forrest Gump?* In the movie, the main character, Forrest Gump, has a very strong point of view. In fact, the entire movie is told from his point of view. You can see where he stands on life, love, and running. This is what you are looking for in a character, even if it is not written in first person point of view.

There are so many screenplays that lack this concept. These are the ones that often get tossed out because no one wants to be confused for ninety minutes. They want to be able to easily follow the character.

Some scenes are drawn out longer than necessary because the character does not have a strong point of view, which causes the scenes to run around in circles. This makes it harder to follow, and more confusing for the audiences that you may have.

A test to see if you are heading in the right direction is to see if you could cut the scene down to no more than two pages. While some scenes need a lot of dialogue, there are still ways to cut it down to make those two pages, and if you cannot do that, then perhaps you have to reevaluate the scene and the character's strength in their point of view. It is best to do this in the editing stages to see what needs to be changed.

What else can we do?

There is no set formula for how to write a character, but if you follow these tips, you will be off to a good start. It is important that you find what works for you because you have to have a solid character for your storyline to move forward.

In fact, all of your characters need to be strong, so that they move the story along smoothly. A bad character is like a speed bump. It interrupts a steady pace and can be frustrating if there is a lot of them.

There are other tips that you can find from other writers as well. Spend some time with your local writer's guild, or go to the library. This will help you immensely to find yourself and find the character you are looking to create. You have to have a solid grasp on your character, for them to flourish.

Go out in the world, and people watch. You can get some ideas for character traits you would like to have in a character. Walmart, the mall, the park. These are all great places to find interesting characters.

Chapter 4: Creating a Rough Draft

Most contracts that you enter into will give you three months maximum from the pitch to come up with a rough draft. Three months may seem like a good amount of time, but it is actually not a lot of time. You have to work swiftly, and efficiently to get your rough draft out in time. Otherwise, you may lose your shot.

Something that helps is to remember that screenplays are time-related. While a novel can be as long or as short as you would like, most feature films run between ninety minutes and two hours. This makes it harder, and easier at the same time. It gives you an idea of how many pages to write but also makes it that much more restrictive to write with a deadline, and a page limit as well. You want to make sure that you streamline the process, to make things go a lot easier.

Getting a good workflow will give you a good storyline. You do not want to seem like you rushed the development. Here are some ideas for a good workflow.

Develop the story idea:

Before you can come up with a story, you must first start with an idea. You cannot just slap words on a page and call it a screenplay. Go somewhere that inspires you, and get an idea for the story from start to finish.

Create the pitch:

Then you have to create the pitch that will give you an idea of how the story will flow. Start with the five finger pitch. This is where you list some major events on one hand. These events once explained should flow nicely. If they do not go do some more thinking. If they do, then you can move on to the two-handed pitch which is just more events that flow smoothly. Once this is complete, you have a solid foundation for your storyline.

Give it structure:

This is like adding the walls to a house. You have to add more turning points, and supporting events. You want to be able to hold the story up, and by giving it structure, then you can have a full blown story coming your way soon.

The importance of structure is that it keeps the entire story from just falling apart at the seams. If you do not have a strong structure of your house, it will fall down. Same with a story.

Build a full story:

Also known as a synopsis, this is where you get all of the major events mapped out. Basically, the synopsis is a one page summary of the entire story. It is the story without all of the minor details and dialogue. Once this is done, you can move onto the next step, which brings you closer to actually writing the rough draft.

Create a beat sheet:

This is a basic outline that will help you keep track of where the story is at, and where it will go next. The outline does not need to be really detailed, it is just a little bullet point list that you can check off as you pass each point in your writing once you finally get to writing your script.

The importance of a beat sheet is to ensure that you are keeping up with the storyline, and moving at the proper pace. Otherwise, you will find that you are stuck, and being stuck can cost you precious time.

Write the script (finally):

Woohoo! It is finally time to get to script writing. You have to make sure that your outline is complete first, and then you can get down to business. There are a lot of software out there that will help you, as they already have the formatting ready for you. Some also have tips and tricks for writing a good script as well. If you are not sure of your abilities, there are software out there that will proofread your script as well for you, though they are a little more costly.

As you are writing, you may find that you need to tweak what you had previously written. Do not go deleting anything yet, instead, create a list of things that need to be fixed, and when you go to edit your rough draft afterward, then you can create an edited rough draft later on. This way you can keep things on track, and get your first rough draft punched out.

Do not delete your original rough draft. It should be kept as your first draft in case you need to go back and reference changes. Once you have edited all of the additional things into your script, you can celebrate.

NEXT STEPS:

The next step is to get your rough draft to the company you have a contract with. They will look it over, and tell you if they like it, and what they feel needs work. Then you can get to editing.

Chapter 5: Editing a Screenplay

Have you ever wondered why a character is rarely seen eating, drinking water, or going to the bathroom unless it has significance to the storyline? The reason these things are rarely portrayed is that this would be too much information, and would drag the story on too long.

In any storytelling form, you have to edit the life of a character in some way. This will keep the storyline moving, and keep it from getting tedious. Bathroom breaks, minor incidences, and repetitive action are generally not important in a storyline, so if you have too much of these, they should be edited out.

Before a screenplay is produced, there are many ways a writer can edit their screenplays. Whether it be through editing and rearranging scenes, juxtaposition, and cutting the fat. All of these are resources that will help the editing process move forward.

Juxtaposition is important to use in any form of art, and screenwriting does not escape its grasp. Just by changing the juxtaposition of scenes, you can give the story an entirely different feel.

This can be used in one scene or two scenes, or depending on how many you need to use it on to help get the point across.

Crosscut and parallel action are two points of juxtaposition that are most commonly used in writing, and they are found to be very effective in creating different tones for different scenes, which is what writers want to achieve.

For instance, a very fun moment cut directly into a boring moment can accentuate that boredom through contrast.

Juxtaposition is a word that is not overlooked in any editing class. It is useful in so many areas, from writing to cinematography, and stage preparation. Prop work as well. The contrast it creates can be useful in setting a tone and creating a mood. This makes it less necessary for words to set the tone, which will leave you more words for important things.

Sometimes, you get so attached to your story that you do not want to cut anything, but the unnecessary parts are important to cut because they just slow the production down. It is important to cut them before they get to production if possible because you do not want to waste more time than you absolutely have to.

Some directors are more spontaneous though. They want you to leave it all in, and they will see how it works as it is being filmed. However, if you cannot get a scene to work when you are writing it, it is still best to leave it out.

However, if you are lower budget, you should make all of the necessary cuts before production, because any delays can cost a lot of money. If you do not have that much money, to begin with, then you will have a hard time recovering.

Removing weaker scenes do not just help production, they help the budget as well. Every page of the script costs money, and if you cut the weaker scenes that wouldn't make the cut anyway, then you save the money it would take to produce them.

Cutting scenes post-production also causes a lot of problems with continuity in a piece as well, because there is not enough time to smooth out the edges.

The continuity of a film is really important. Without that continuity, it will feel like someone gave a twelve-year-old a camera and told them to make a movie.

It is important to take the lighting into consideration as well. Consider how the light will affect the mood. So when editing, you have to pay close attention to the lighting to make sure it stays consistent. Fix it if you need to because the wrong lighting could set the wrong mood, which would shut your whole production down. If you do not want that you will make sure to specify the time of day in every scene.

Not only does the light change, but your character may also change as well. If a lot of time progresses, your character cannot stay the same the entire time. You have to make sure that you have made note of the changes as the film progresses.

The visuals are usually clear-cut, but if scenes need to be cut in post-production, that can disrupt the visuals. If several scenes need cut, then you may find that certain scenes need to be reshot to fix the visuals. This is another reason to focus on editing closely.

When editing, it is important to keep in mind the order of the scenes to ensure that the continuity is there. If something needs to be switched around, make sure to adjust it accordingly, so that the visuals are smooth, and there are no visual speed bumps when you hit production. Because it becomes a lot harder to fix on the spot then, and you want a smooth transition to have a successful film. Visuals are very important, and it is important to remember that.

Another part of editing is to make sure that you note the transitions. Every film has to have transitions between scenes so that they flow smoothly. Otherwise, you would have to add a whole lot more information. These transitions are a lot easier to add in the editing process than the post-production days. So make sure to make a note of the transitions before it becomes harder to add them.

Another reason to make sure everything is solid in editing is that there can be unwanted interpretations if you have to cut scenes in post-production. Doing so between similar scenes can create confusion, and doing so between contrasting scenes can be jarring and dramatic. This can be used to say something if it is intentional. However, if it is not intentional, you risk saying something to the audience that you never meant to say, which can leave them confused.

Also, directors do not like to be told how to do their job, so avoid technical directions in your script. Instead be subtle in telling the director where the camera should be pointed. Instead of saying "Point camera to the west." You could say "The main character looked off into a beautiful sunset, contemplating the meaning of life. Since the sun sets in the west, the camera will point west.

Editing can save you from a lot of issues later on in life and ensures smoother transitions as you head into production. It is important to make sure you edit out all of the kinks to save money when it comes time to shoot the film. Now if only taxes could be edited out of our lives.

Chapter 6: Tips for Success

While there are a wide variety of reasons that you might want to be a screenwriter, if you are hoping to do so in order to adopt a shorter, less stressful, work week you may be extremely disappointed. In fact, successful screenwriters are often extremely disciplined, dedicated individuals who have trained themselves to create something from nothing, day end and day out in order to ensure they always have something productive in the pipeline. While what works out to be an effective process for each writer is going to differ, sometimes dramatically, the most successful all typically have a number of habits in common that make the task before them more manageable. These are outlined here, in hopes that at least a few of them will inspire you to write more successfully in the future.

They have a reason to write: The best screenplays, especially those written by first time screenwriters are written with a specific purpose in mind, by writers with a driving desire to tell a specific story. This doesn't mean that your motivations for telling your story need to be pure as the driven snow, after all, entertaining others is as good of reason as any. The important thing is that you have a reason that is strong enough to drive you to continue trying to tell your story no matter how hard the going is going to get, and it is likely to be quite difficult from time to time.

Regardless of the motives that you have for writing, you need to be passionate about it if you ever hope to find true success. Don't feel ashamed if part of the reason that you want to write a successful screenplay has something to do with egotism, remember, the goal isn't to make yourself want to write a screenplay that will change the world, it is to find what drives you to write, and in this case egotism is as useful of a reason as any. Everyone wants recognition to some degree, and if you want to write for revenge, glory, fame, money, power, or simply to prove that you can, then you can harness that energy and use to make you a better writer, ensuring you actually see the screenplay through in the process.

They demand the best from themselves: When you first start writing your screenplay, it is perfectly acceptable to leave in placeholder scenes and text, from time to time, just to ensure you make it through to the end in one piece. With that being said, it is important to keep in mind that the spec script your produce is going to be the one, and often only, thing that people in the industry look at when they decide if they are going to give you your big break which means that settling for anything less that absolute perfection is akin to throwing away all the time that you ultimately spend on your screenplay.

As such, it is important to never settle with your first draft, your second or even your fourth. You are going to want to go through the entire thing with a fine-tooth comb until the story is as tight and compelling as possible. While this is only going to ever take you so far, it will at least ensure that the screenplay that you send in is the most accurate indication of what you are capable of as possible.

At the same time, you are going to want to make a conscious effort to stop making changes at the point where the work, as presented, speaks for itself as you can always find something to tweak or change. Eventually you are going to need to have the confidence in yourself to put the work out there and, hopefully, start receiving feedback on it. If you don't practice restraint, your screenplay will likely end up feeling overwrought, as you will have overthought whatever spark was there to begin with into oblivion.

They write what they like, and what they know: While anyone can have an idea for any type of story, and that story might be unique, or relatable, enough to resonate with the world at large, you will typically find that it is much easier to write about things that you have first-hand knowledge about and also much easier to keep at it if you like whatever it is that you are writing. Again, it is perfectly acceptable to get into the screenwriting business for its potential for lucrative gains, this in no way means that you can't enjoy the process along the way. What's more, if you find the story in your screenplay exciting, the odds are high that those around you are going to feel the same way.

Likewise, when it comes to writing what you know, this doesn't mean writing a movie about being an accountant for an accounting firm, unless you have an idea that will make the process seem roughly 2,000 percent more exciting than the topic naturally seems to the average person. Rather, adding in touches from your every day life can make certain characters more believable, or giving one of your hobbies to a character can make them seem more three-dimensional. What's more, you never know when something from, even a seemingly boring job, can provide you with the one realistic, but unexpected, fact that you need to tie the whole plot together.

They set goals: If you have never before found yourself sitting in front of a blank screen, with all the freedom in the world in front of you, only to find yourself looking for any excuse to be anywhere else, then the idea of setting writing goals to ensure you actually finish your screenplay may seem unnecessary. The first time you make the decision to bolt rather than face down your writer's block, however, you will realize just how vital setting goals can be. Likewise, if you have never written anything substantial before, then you may find yourself doing all the research you need to complete your screenplay, only to find that you never actually get any closer to generating a truly finished product.

As such, you should start by setting goals for your pre-writing process, including generating characters, a basic plot synopsis, world building elements etc. You should give yourself plenty of time for the more free-form nature of this part of the process, though you should have a firm deadline when you want to begin the actual writing to ensure that fleshing out your characters doesn't end up taking years to finish.

When it comes to writing the first draft, you are going to want to make a concentrated effort to write for at least an hour a day, at least five days a week, and also spend some time on the sixth day coming up with a general idea of where the end of the next week should find you. Writing every day will help to ensure that you don't lose the flow of the story as it can be hard to recapture lost momentum once it has slipped away. While writing for a set period of time is fine, you will find that you will be more productive still if you task yourself with writing a set number of pages each day. This will ensure that you maintain your productivity, rather than just waiting out the clock on days where inspiration takes longer to strike. In addition to page goals, you are going to want to have a general idea of where you want to the story to go next, so you can steer things in that direction.

When it comes to editing, you are going to want to set hourly goals, as it is difficult to say just how much work you will get done per session as it is going to vary so dramatically. When it comes to setting an overall timeline for completion, you are going to want to give yourself enough time to ensure you don't rush, but not so much that you don't feel obligated to make daily progress. When setting these goals, it is important to keep in mind that they are not taking place in a vacuum. Writing for three or four hours every day is an admirable goal, and likely one that is completely unrealistic if you already have a fulltime job. It is important to set goals that are achievable as failing to do so can harm your morale and making finishing your screenplay harder than it already is.

Finally, the overall length of your timeline isn't important, as there is no standard amount of time it should take to create a quality screenplay. The most important thing overall, is that setting a schedule will help you to make finishing your screenplay a priority which means you are going to be far more likely to finish it than you otherwise would. Remember, your screenplay could be your shot at the bigtime, but the only way you will ever know for sure is if you actually finish it.

Conclusion

Hopefully, you learned a lot about writing a screenplay from this book. It was filled with plenty of tips on how to proceed. This is important because you cannot just jump in.

Now, you can go out, and start working on your screenplay. This book can be your guide if you whenever get stuck.

Thank you and good luck!

STORY STRUCTURE

STEP-BY-STEP

ESSENTIAL STORY BUILDING, STORY
DEVELOPMENT AND SUSPENSE WRITING
TRICKS ANY WRITER CAN LEARN

SANDY MARSH

BOOK 2: STORY STRUCTURE

STEP-BY-STEP

Essential Story Building, Story Development and Suspense Writing Tricks Any Writer Can Learn

Sandy Marsh

reparation, damages, or monetary loss due to the information herein, either directly or indirectly.

Respective authors own all copyrights not held by the publisher.

The information herein is offered for informational purposes solely, and is universal as so. The presentation of the information is without contract or any type of guarantee assurance.

The trademarks that are used are without any consent, and the publication of the trademark is without permission or backing by the trademark owner. All trademarks and brands within this book are for clarifying purposes only and are the owned by the owners themselves, not affiliated with this document.

Table of Contents

Introduction

Thank you and congratulations on purchasing *"Story Structure: Step-by-Step | Essential Story Building, Story Development and Suspense Writing Tricks Any Writer Can Learn"*.

This book was created to help you learn a series of tips and tricks that will help you enrich your story and make it a must-read book for your target audience. By using these techniques and strategies in your own book you will be able to generate a storyline that is rich with suspense, action, and other tools that are important to keep your readers engaged and excited about reading your book.

Each chapter within' this book is dedicated to one element of story structures themselves, ensuring that you are provided with the greatest in-depth detail to ensure that you learn plenty to help you produce a phenomenal story. Before the book ends, you will be provided with tips from top writers and authors that will help you write like the pros.

This book was not designed for any particular experience level when it comes to writing. Instead, it has been populated with tricks that will help any writer from beginner to advanced. If you are someone who typically struggles to write stories but you are looking to get yours heard, you can be certain that you will learn some tips here to help you get on your way towards having your book completed. Likewise, if you have done this before but are looking for a refresher or are otherwise interested in learning more to enrich your story and create an addictive read for your audience, you are certainly going to learn something also.

Please be sure to take your time and work through all of the tips and tricks provided within' this book. While some may not be entirely relevant to the work you are producing, they may provide you with inspiration to move forward in a more powerful way. As well, be sure to keep this book handy for future writing ventures as you never know which part will stand out each time. Finally, remember that writing is an experience that should be enjoyed by both the reader and the author. Be sure that you take the time to make the process enjoyable for yourself so that you can produce your best work. And finally, have fun!

Chapter 1: Purpose of Story Structure

Understanding the purpose of story structure will ensure that you are aware of how it can make (or break) your story, and why it is so crucial that you develop a strong structure within' your own story. Prior to diving into any important tips or strategies, we are going to explore what a story structure is, exactly, and what purpose it serves within' your story.

What is a Story Structure?

In basic form, a story structure is essentially a map that is drawn to take your reader from point a to point b. You want them to start at the beginning of the book and end at the end, only after being taken through an experience which is essentially each "stop" on the map. This map is used to help identify how people solve different problems, as well as to assist in conveying the message that the author is attempting to send from the storytelling process. In essence, the structure of your story is the process where the outline is transformed from being a simple idea to being the bones of your story. It becomes the part that holds the entire story up and gives it a form that is both natural, yet moving.

Where do Story Structures Come from?

Story structure is less of an invention or creation and more of an element of the story that was observed and thus plucked from the process and used as a tool to help generate new stories. For thousands of years, humans have been telling stories to one another whilst using story structure without ever knowing what it actually was. This is the part of the story that was used to draw listeners or readers forward through the story while keeping them actively engaged and wanting to know more. With the use of story structure, storytellers were able to walk people through the process of the story, rather than simply telling them the beginning and end factors. This meant that storytelling became an experience, both for the teller and the listener or reader. It was all thanks to story structure.

Although people weren't aware of what story structure actually was in the beginning, the idea of it emerged over time. It was identified as the structure of the story that was used to describe how certain characters within' the story dealt with problems and overcame them, as well as how they interacted with and communicated with other individuals from the story.

After identifying the concept of story structure and observing it from ancient storytelling experiences, people began using it as a general guideline for the process of building stories. Now, your story structure involves important information about the setting of your story, the people involved, the conflicts they experience, and how they overcome said conflicts. It is essentially every part of your story pulled together and planned out in a specific structure that helps you as the author understand what story you are trying to tell before and during the writing process.

Why You Need One

Having a story structure may seem pointless, especially if you already have the story in your head and you are simply attempting to get it out on paper. However, story structures are extremely valuable and can help you with the entire storytelling process. They are excellent for helping you identify how you are going to deliver the story to ensure that the reader receives the story effectively. This is more than simply providing the reader with information to help walk them from point a to point b. Instead, it is about giving them this relevant information in such a way that they are eager to know more and they stay actively engaged with the storytelling process.

When you design your story structure it helps you identify what your story sounds like to other people when they are reading it. It is important that you develop one before you start writing so that you have a strong execution plan going into the writing process. While you can simply write the story from your mind, this may result in you not emphasizing strong points enough, or otherwise diluting your story with information that takes away from it having a strong structure. Instead, you could plan your story out on paper first and essentially lay out the points that you will take your readers through within' the story. This way you can walk yourself through it and learn more about your story in advance. Doing this gives you the opportunity to identify any weak points and strengthen them, to ensure that your story makes sense and flows well, and to develop confidence in the idea that you have generated a strong enough plotline that your readers are going to stay actively engaged and enjoy the reading experience.

Now that you are more clear on what a story structure is and why it is so crucial to the writing process, it is time to explore the process of actually creating your own story structure so that you can embark on writing your own story. The following chapters will walk you through the step-by-step process of building your own story structure, as well as every technique you should know in order to have a strong structure that will leave your readers wanting more.

Chapter 2: The Essentials of Building a Structure

The first part of generating your own story structure is understanding the essentials. In this chapter, we are going to explore all of the basics that you should know when it comes to creating your own story structure. Throughout this chapter, you will be provided with tips and techniques to help you design the foundation of your structure. By the end, you should have a solid structure that will help you produce a phenomenal story.

9 Step Process

Most stories follow a typical nine-step process in order to generate their story structure. Some people prefer to alternate how the structure is designed, such as by introducing the climax in the first portion of the book. Still, they typically tend to break the book up into three main parts, or "acts" as they are called. This helps keep each part of the book focused on a certain subject that ultimately contributes to the overall story.

The following sections will introduce each step of the nine-step process and how they should be executed in order to produce a high-quality story structure. Please note that these are following the traditional method based on how many other stories have been structured throughout the ages. You may choose to alternate yours if you are more advanced, but if you are new to storytelling you will likely want to stick to and master this traditional structure before venturing into other structures. This will provide you with more practice towards developing a structure and using the purpose of the structure to your advantage. Once you are more skilled with structures then you can start to create alternative ones for your future stories because you will have a stronger idea about what makes them work and what doesn't.

Step One: First Act

The first step is to introduce the first act. This is the part of the story where you want to introduce the reader to your characters, the setting you have chosen, and anything that is at stake in the story. This is where they understand what is important and why. In the first act, you are given the opportunity to catch the attention of the reader and give them a reason to care about what story you are telling.

Example: You are writing a romance novel so you introduce the two lovers, as well as any other important characters to the reader. You will also take the time to provide insight as to where the book is taking place. This is where you can introduce the stakes as well, which essentially means you are telling the reader what is at stake and why it is important to the protagonist.

Step Two: The First Major Plot Point

The second step is to introduce the first major plot point to your reader. This should be defined by an event that takes place which forces the character to take action. You want this first major plot point to be considered the last scene in the first act so that readers are left wanting more. This is the finale of the first part of your book, so you want to leave it with some form of small cliffhanger. This both rewards the reader for reading by giving them some action to pay attention to, but also has them wondering what is going to come next as a result of the character's actions.

Example: The female character in your romance novel is walking home when an attacker tries to hurt her. The male character comes seemingly from nowhere and defends her honor, ensuring that she was protected and was not harmed by the attacker.

Step Three: First Half of Second Act

This is the part of the book where your character is coming back from the action they took at the end of the first act. Here you further explain what happened as a result of that plot point, as well as how your characters are dealing with it.

Example: As a result of him being the first to hit the attacker, despite him attempting to defend the female, the male role in your novel is being subjected to a criminal investigation. Because of this, he is trying to keep a low profile and avoid any further complications. The female is angry with the male for not calling the cops instead and allowing them to deal with it. She is upset that he has subjected himself to the criminal investigation through his actions, regardless of his reasoning.

Step Four: Second Major Plot Point

This is a plot point within' the story where the character who was attempting to regain their bearings from the first major plot point is forced back into action. Here, you want to work together with what said character has at stake to help the reader understand why they have been forced into action. Often the action is forced unto the character in the form of an ultimatum.

Example: Despite keeping a low profile for some time, the attacker returns and attempts to strike again. Only this time, he knows that the male is with the female and the attacker is attempting to force the male to act. He wants to have the male punished for attacking him, regardless of the fact that he was only attempting to protect her from the attacker. As a result, the male role is forced to decide between protecting her again or being faced with serious jail time. For the sake of these examples, let's say that he chooses to defend her honor once again.

Step Five: Second Half of Second Act

This is the part where all of the characters in the story begin to come into their own. Here, they are all grouping together to come against the antagonist. They are ensuring that the initial character is no longer left to take action on his or her own, but rather that they are supported by the other characters within' the story.

Example: This time, the female character is aware of what is going on and she is fighting to protect the male character. She is no longer angry with him for making the choice he made originally, and she is more willing to testify in his defense. They work together to get the attacker in trouble and to protect the male character through pleading that he was only practicing self-defense.

Step Six: Third Major Plot Point

This is where the protagonist's behavior appears to have led him or her to a place of defeat. In this part of the story, you want to introduce the idea that there may be no hope for this character and that they may be doomed because of the antagonistic forces. Here, they are beginning to feel as though they have hit rock bottom.

Example: Despite the female character testifying to the male character and fighting in his corner this time around, the court orders him guilty for assault. It appears that even though he was attempting to protect himself and the female character, no one is willing to see that. It seems there is no hope for him to avoid criminal charges altogether.

Step Seven: Third Act

In the third act, the protagonist is fighting against the antagonistic force as a last effort to take them down. Here they may not have total confidence that they can do it but they are not willing to give up just yet.

Example: The male character chooses to appeal the court ruling. Together, he and the female work to create a plan where they will prove that he is innocent and the attacker is the one who is truly guilty.

Step Eight: Climax

This is where there is a final face-off between the protagonist and antagonist. This is the deciding moment that is responsible for determining whether the story will end in favor of the antagonist, or in favor of the protagonist.

Example: The male character and the attacker face off in court. This is the part of the story that will determine whether the male is ruled guilty and is no longer welcome to appeal the charges, or whether the judge will see that he is actually innocent and it is the attacker who should be facing charges. For the sake of the example, we will say that it ends with the attacker being charged and the male being let off.

Step Nine: Resolution

This is where any loose ends from the story. It will also give insight to how the characters react to the climax and where they end up afterward. This is the wind down where readers are given the opportunity to know "what's next" and is required to avoid you from ending your book in a cliff-hanger.

Example: The female character is ecstatic that the male character is let free and they decide that they never want to risk facing a life without the other so they choose to get married.

As you can see, developing a strong story structure is important. Hopefully, through the use of the examples, you were able to understand how the structure lent a hand towards generating suspense and giving the reader a reason to keep reading. Because of how the story was structured and when certain pieces of information were revealed, the individual reading the story once it was complete would be engaged and would thus stay committed to reading the entire story so that they could discover how it ended.

It is important that you pay attention to the book in three sections as outlined above, as well as that you have a major plot point in each part. Dividing your story into three sections ensures that each part focuses on a particular element of the story and avoids you from going back and forth or otherwise introducing elements that are later forgotten about because you are not clear and focused on what you are writing. Having a major plot point in each section ensures that each section is rich and your reader is engaged the entire time. This is ultimately the structure you need in order to draw your reader forward and keep them moving through the story until they reach the end.

Chapter 3: Developing Your Story

Now that you are aware of what it takes to design a strong story structure, you may be wondering how you can develop a story that will fit with the structure! If you already have a general idea, then you can use the information from this section to help you strengthen that idea and ensure that all areas of your story are considered before them being structured and then written. If you have no idea as to what your story is going to be yet, use this chapter to help you identify a story and develop it so that it provides you with plenty of material to write your book about.

Study Existing Plots

When you are working towards developing your story one of the best ways to go about it is to read. Reading other people's stories gives you the opportunity to see what worked and what didn't, and it also provides you with inspiration to enrich your own story. While you don't want to be plagiarizing or stealing stories from other people, getting inspiration to enrich your own and strengthen the plot is always a great idea. This ensures that you are going to have a really strong story that provides enough material to engage your audience and keep them captive for the duration of the book.

When you are studying other people's stories you want to do more than just read them. You want to pay attention to who the characters are, how they develop throughout the novel, how the events take place including when and where, and all locations that the story takes place in. You should also identify the sequence that the locations are used in. Knowing more about these primary areas of the story allows you to get an idea of how books are written and what authors do in order to develop their own storyline. You can see the techniques in action and understand how they contribute to the overall experience being delivered in the story.

Draft Up Your Plot

When you are designing your plot there are some strategies you can use to see your plot come together without writing out the entire story first. The best way to do this is through drafting up your plot. You can do this by writing a paragraph or two from each ideal chapter and then read them in order. While it will obviously be missing many details, doing this will give you an idea of how the plot points flow together and if they are strong enough to give you plenty of writing material to work with.

Using a plotting strategy like this gives you the opportunity to look at your plot as a whole and make sure that it works effectively in the story you are writing. This helps you see what areas of the plot are rich and which aren't. You can also finalize the main plot sequencing and points before starting the writing process so that you are certain that it is in the order that you want and that it all works well together. This essentially gives you a birds-eye view of what your structure is and lets you know whether or not it works.

Create a Timeline

A great way to build your story is to create a timeline. This timeline should include all of the major plot points in chronological order. Seeing these together helps you identify how each one builds into the next one and makes sure that they work well together. If anything is missing or you feel there is a plot point that does not fit well in the overall story, then you can use this as an opportunity to eliminate it.

Similar to drafting your plot, creating a timeline allows you to take a birds-eye view at the work you have created and determine whether or not it works. The more you pay attention to the structure of your story from different elements now, the more you can be certain that it will work and produce a strong story in the long run.

Plan Character Development Along the Plot Line

After you have generated your plot draft and your timeline, take your characters into consideration. Pay attention to how you want them to develop along the storyline. It is natural for characters to change throughout stories, and even necessary in order for the story to progress. A great way to plan their development is to plan it alongside the story development. How is the development of the story going to contribute to the growth of the character? Consider this while you are deciding how your character will develop along the way.

Change the 5 "W's

A great way to ensure that you have developed the story strong enough is to check that you have changed the five w's along the way. The who, what, when, where, and why of the story should all develop or completely change along the progression of your story. In real life, these change from moment to moment and day to day. If you want your story to be realistic and relatable, you need to ensure that they are changed in your story as well.

If you want to take your story from good to great, these answers should not be simple and direct. Each one should have a series of answers that guide the element from the start of the book to the end. They should change in a way that convinces the reader that the change was natural and realistic, and helps the character feel as though it is a true story being told. Think back to your own day, for example you may have woken up in your home and now you are sitting in a coffee shop reading this book. You may have woken in a bad mood and now you are in a better one, or vice versa. The reasons as to why your mood change are also important to the story of your day. Who was involved in your day and what helped you pass the day by will have also changed from moment to moment. Just like your day naturally progressed as a story of its own, you need your story to progress in the same way. This ensures that your book goes in-depth enough to make it convincing to your reader. If any of the five w's are not developed enough, look for opportunities to strengthen them so that your story will be rich and full of realistic details.

Design a Story Board

Creating a storyboard is another great way to look at the structure of your story. A great way to create the storyboard is to write each major plot point and important element on a cue card or post it so that they can easily be moved around to create the final story map. This gives you a great opportunity to see how each event works together and organize them effortlessly without having to scratch out things and replace them everywhere.

Consider Subplots

Creating subplots that fit in seamlessly with your overall story is a great way to enrich the story experience and add more depth to it while also encouraging reader engagement. Subplots are essentially the "what else" part of the story. For example, if you are writing a book about the main character who is seeking justice, consider including elements of why this justice is so important for this character. Perhaps they want the criminal incarcerated because he or she deserves to be, but it may also be because the protagonist has allowed others to walk all over him for too long and he is ready to stand up for himself. Therefore, getting justice is both about having justice served *and* about building the confidence to actually fight for what is right.

Subplots are an incredible story developing strategy that can help you create a story that is much richer in context. You can include as many or as few subplots as you want, but make sure that each one makes sense to the overall story itself. They should work together with the main plot, rather than going against it or straying away from it completely.

Incorporate Driven Elements

All of the best stories incorporate one specific element that enables the story to be so great. That is the element of change. In order to create change, there are two very specific things you need. Character-driven and action-driven elements to your story. These elements are two things that can help incorporate change into your story in such a way that yours fosters all of the greatness that all of the other best titles do.

The reason why change is so powerful in a story is that that is what drives the story forward. People are curious to know about how characters change and grow throughout the course of the story every bit as much as they are interested in learning about how the story develops itself. People do not want to read a story about static characters who do the same thing every day and nothing changes. That would be extremely boring and would lead to them closing the book and turning away from it entirely. Think about it, would you read a book like that? Likewise, people are not interested in a book that has minimal change, or where the change only occurs on one very specific thing. Instead, people want to see the entire story change. They want to see the characters grow, they want to see the circumstances evolve, and they want to see the protagonist, and even the antagonist, end up somewhere completely different from where they were when the story changed. Incorporating as much natural and realistic change as possible helps drive your story forward and keep it both interesting and engaging.

As previously mentioned, there are two different types of change you can use to drive your story forward: character-driven change, and action-driven change. Both of these elements should be included in your own story if you want a diverse and realistic story that will help keep your readers engaged and reading your book all the way until the last page.

Character-driven change is used by showing the stakes the character has. For example, their child, their family, their significant other, their career. By incorporating these stakes and giving the reader insight as to why they are so important to the character, you can use them as an opportunity to drive the story forward. The most important thing to understand is that without character-driven change, there is no story. Character-driven change is essentially the answer to "why" your character is doing anything that takes place in the story. This explains why they will do almost anything, even stuff that seems highly irrational or nonsensical, in various situations. "Because my child is sick" or, "because I could lose my job" for example, would be the stakes and therefore would answer "why" the character is so invested in something. By creating this type of explanation and therefore emotional attachment from the reader to the character, and furthermore the character's stakes, you can make virtually every part of the story that much more engaging and interesting for your reader. Without character-driven change, your readers are not given an opportunity to understand why they need to care about the events taking place in your book.

Action-driven change is an entirely different form of change. This is the change whereby specific actions happen that cause the story to drive forward. High-speed chases, break-ins, getting arrested, being put on the chopping block at work, the spouse falling in love with someone else, the kid getting into trouble, all of these would constitute as action-drive changes. For the most part, these are actions that are taking place that cannot be stopped or influenced by your protagonist. Instead, the protagonist must find a way to respond and react to these actions.

When you use character-driven change effectively, action-driven change becomes that much more intriguing and engaging for your reader. Because they understand the stakes and have developed an emotional attachment to your characters, they are much more concerned with the action, as well as the outcome. It is important that you use a balanced amount of both types of changes in your story. This will help you round out your story and keep it moving forward without being too heavily charged in one direction or another. Furthermore, you want to make sure that you don't go overboard on the change. While it does drive the story forward, you want to make sure that you use it in a very realistic and natural manner. This helps the reader relate to the story and believe it, instead of feeling as though it is completely unlikely and therefore it is not relatable. If a reader cannot relate to a story in one way or another, they are not going to continue reading it because it will be too unbelievable for them.

Question Yourself

When you are in the process of developing your story, make sure you question yourself a lot along the way. The more you question yourself, your intentions, the story and the plot line, the more you can develop it. Questioning it ultimately gives you the opportunity to see where any loopholes may lie, if any part of the plot is weak, or if there is any reason that you should need to develop part of the story more. It also helps you identify where there may be too much action or development going on so that you can scale it back. If you are not taking the time to question yourself and your story structure, you may be missing important things that could take away from the value of your story altogether.

Some great questions to ask yourself include ones such as:

- Why has the character changed, how did the change happen, and what was the purpose of this change?

- How much has the character changed since the beginning of the story?

- Is the change natural and believable?

- What has each plot point taught the characters, thus teaching them about the story's primary situation or conflict?

- Can you identify some core themes within' the story? Are there too many or too few core themes taking place?

- Is the story believable? Does it flow naturally?

- Does the story move forward effectively, or is it too slow?

Asking yourself these questions will help ensure that each part of your story structure is strong and that it will help you produce a believable, relatable, and enjoyable story that is interesting and engaging. If you find that your answer is "no" or "I don't know" to any of the questions above, take the time to further explore that question and find ways that you can strengthen the story structure itself.

Get Feedback

Finally, it is important that you take the time to get feedback on your story structure. As with most things, having someone else take a look and give you some insight as to where the strengths and weaknesses lie and if any adaptations or alterations should be made means that nothing will be missed. This is the best way to make sure that you have a strong structure going into your story that will both serve you and serve your readers by giving you enough material and answers to generate an interesting an engaging story.

If you do not personally know someone who can provide you with feedback, there are many online platforms and forums that you can turn to where you can find someone to help you with looking over the structure. Furthermore, you can also look to find someone from your ideal target audience and have them look over the structure for you. Regardless of who you get to help you with the structure, do your best to make sure it is someone who is either in or thoroughly understands your target audience, and ideally someone with some experience in story structure. Having someone who intimately knows you are trying to reach and what you are trying to say can help significantly as it ensures that any feedback or critique they provide you with is accurate and helpful. Those who are unclear on the audience you are trying to reach or who have zero understanding of story structure or what is required in order to make a good book may not be able to provide you with information that will help you improve your structure. In fact, they may even have you questioning parts that you should not need to question. It is important that the person you choose to work with understands your needs.

Chapter 4: Creating Suspense

Regardless of what genre you are writing for, you need to be skilled in creating suspense for your story. Suspense is the element that keeps readers wondering what is coming next and how events are going to unfold. When used properly, suspense can be what draws one plot point to the next. If you want to create a compelling and convincing fiction novel that encourages readers to continue reading, you are going to need to master the art of creating suspense. The next ten tips are about how you can begin creating suspense in your own novel to keep your readers wanting more.

Understand Your Genre

Before you begin creating suspense, it is important that you understand the genre you are writing in. Each genre uses suspense differently to draw characters forward and keep readers coming back. If you want to do your book justice, you need to practice using suspense for your unique genre.

Let's take a look at three different types of novels and where the suspense would come into play for each type.

Mystery: A horror or major event takes place in the first chapter and the rest of the book is spent figuring out why the event occurred and who was responsible for it. For example, the protagonist's spouse was killed in the first chapter and the rest of the book is spent uncovering who was responsible.

Romance: You build up to the point where the two lovers finally get together. The climax, or the two getting together, officially takes place later in the book, usually within' the last couple of chapters. For example, two lovers know they're meant to be together but the timing never seems right. One is always dating someone else when the other is available for the relationship to work. As a result, they are never able to get together until the end when they finally make it work.

Suspense: The knowledge of an impending horror is upon the characters in the novel and they spend the entire time trying to avoid it until they can no longer keep it from happening. For example, someone knows they are going to jail for embezzlement but doesn't know when. This character knows that he has been tracked and that the FBI is well aware of what has been going on. He does not know when he will be taken down, but it will happen.

Provide Adequate Viewpoints

When it comes to developing a strong case of suspense in your novel, you need to give the reader adequate knowledge. This comes from providing them with different viewpoints. Through this, you can give them insight to the protagonist's side of things, and the antagonist's side of things. The best way to get a lot of suspense building in your book is by giving your reader insight as to what is going to happen before the protagonist knows. This gives the writer the opportunity to increase the emotional attachment to the protagonist and the stakes. The reader is drawn along an experience where they know what is yet to come but they have to watch the protagonist find out and learn the consequences of certain actions. The tension that builds on the reader because of what they know that the protagonist doesn't know is similar to someone who has a secret they're not allowed to tell. It engages the reader and makes them want to know more and to understand where the book will end up.

Put Time on Your Side

Time is an incredible tool when it comes to writing a book with suspense. You want to use time on your side so that you can increase the amount of suspense in the novel. Time gives you the opportunity to make the reader feel as though the protagonist is working against the clock. Everything they are doing should have some form of time constraint on it. Ideally, it should appear as though the clock is working in favor of the antagonist or antagonistic force to keep the suspense strong. For example, if you were writing a mystery novel about a murder that took place, it should seem as though the protagonist doesn't have enough time to find the murderer. Perhaps there is some jurisdiction law that states that if the person is not found within' a set amount of time the charges won't be as strong, or the murderer has been leaving clues that they have left town and it gets harder and harder to find who they are. Several dead end leads are exhausted before the protagonist finally discovers who the murderer was in the end. Putting time on your side lets you build suspense by creating the illusion that something won't happen, even though it needs to.

Keep The Stakes High

The stakes that you use in a story should be high enough to justify a high amount of suspense. The higher the stakes the more pressing the need to protect them is, both in the mind of the character and the reader. While you don't need to choose devastating stakes that are excessively high, picking ones that someone would actually be desperate to protect will ensure that your reader understands why the protagonist is so passionate about protecting their stakes. Some examples would include an executive who is facing being exposed for shady business dealings, therefore costing them their job and their reputation and making them unlikeable for other employers. Or, perhaps a male is in love with a female in a romance novel, but he grows tired of waiting for her to make up her mind so he pursues a relationship with someone else. She realizes she wants him more than anything but must figure out a way to tell him, and fast, before he marries the other person or realizes that he does not want to be with her altogether. Alternatively, you may choose to write a story about someone with a powerful societal position being murdered and they must find out who did it before they strike another powerful member of society. By keeping the stakes high but reasonable, you make it very clear as to why your reader needs to be so concerned with what is taking place in the book. The stronger your stakes are, the more your reader will be passionate alongside your character to ensure that they are not lost.

Don't Be Afraid to Apply Pressure

Pressure is a great way to add suspense to any novel. The odds should be stacked well against your character and it should take a great amount of effort and energy for them to tip the odds in their favor and save the day. The more the odds are stacked against them, the higher the pressure is and therefore the more you can draw the reader to wondering if they will ever be able to beat the odds. When they finally do, the reader and character alike will feel a great deal of relief from the experience.

When you are writing about creating pressure, make sure that you never lead your protagonist right to the breaking point. They should bend and cripple under pressure, but they should never stop pushing. You should ensure that they are always pushed *almost* too far so that they have *just* enough amount of energy to push back and it is at that time that they finally beat the antagonistic force and experience success in their heroic attempts.

Make Use of Dilemmas

Dilemmas are a great way to increase suspense in a story and have your reader highly engaged. Dilemmas present a "this or that" action for the character. They should be forced into action, and make sure that the pressure is on for it to happen fast. When dilemmas are being thrown towards your character it is important to make sure that they are being thrown by the antagonist most often. This should present the idea that the protagonist cannot win in the situation. For example, for them to save one character another must die, they can either lose their family and save their job or lose their job and save their family, or even indulging in alcohol after swearing to sobriety at some point within' the novel.

When you are presenting dilemmas, make sure that the antagonist always crosses the line. Because they are the villain, they shouldn't even think twice about going across it. However, the protagonist should always be forced with their morals and values. Should they do one, or the other? Which will be the less of two evils? Is there a way that they can make the best of both horrible situations? True to heroic nature, they should be struggling to find the answer to the dilemma.

One great reason why dilemmas work is because you can apply pressure and time constraints so that the protagonist is forced to make a decision fast, which puts pressure on him and gets the reader worried about what is going to happen. Using these three strategies together is a great way to build suspense throughout your book.

Complicate Things

You don't need to restrict to just presenting your protagonist with one or even two conflicts at any given time. Instead, feel free to pile on the complications every now and again. The more complicated things get, the more difficult it will be for them to come up with the solution and make the right choice. At times, it should feel like the protagonist is trying to juggle several balls at once and he is just barely keeping them from dropping every time. This is a great time to push the protagonist almost to the point of breaking before bringing them back in for a final and much awaited victory.

Avoid Becoming Predictable

When your book runs too smoothly, it becomes predictable. It also becomes uninteresting and the readers struggle to relate to it. Life is not about being smooth and predictable. Most often we are all living in a hot mess where we are balancing many different things and trying to stay afloat along the way. If you want to write a great book, it should be similar to this. Throw random curveballs in, take a spin somewhere where one wasn't expected, and have your reader surprised at some of the elements that are being tossed in, and when. When it comes to writing, don't let the hero rely on the idea that everything will go in their favor. In fact, almost nothing should. This way when it finally does, it will come as a surprise. Furthermore, your antagonist shouldn't go with everything going in their way, either. Let both of them face challenges, twists and turns along the way. The more they are affected by curveballs and unexpected experiences, the more realistic the story will be. Make the protagonist slip up and result in an almost-victory instead of a true victory, and let the antagonist fail at the most inconvenient of times for them. This keeps your readers on their toes and unsure about what is going to happen, when.

Develop Your Villain

Your villain is the antagonistic force in your book, and they need to be developed really well. Your reader should be mentally pushing against the villain, and rooting for the hero. As a result, you need to have a really well developed villain that has the reader truly believing and feeling as though they are a nasty force to be reckoned with.

Make sure that you use the right villain for your novel genre, as well. In a mystery, for example, it should not be clear as to who the villain is until the end. With a romance novel on the other hand, the villain might be time itself, or the person coming between the two lovers and keeping them apart. Alternatively, in a suspense novel the villain should be highly visible at all times and people should ultimately just be wondering when they will finally strike. The more you understand what type of villain is appropriate for your unique genre, the easier it will be to create one that is believable and extremely well developed.

When you develop your antagonist, make sure that you are very specific on who they are and what makes them tick. You want this character to be so developed that your reader feels as though they personally know them. Furthermore, your antagonist should change throughout the story, which is easiest to prove if your reader knows who they are from how you've written about them.

Develop Your Hero

In addition to developing your villain, you need to develop your hero. This is the one that finally defeats the antagonistic force and creates the victory of the story. The best way to create a strong hero is to really build on the character and give the reader plenty of reasons to love them. This is the character your reader is going to follow throughout the story. This is who they will be rooting for, worrying for, and curious about. They want to know everything they can about this character, and they have mentally prepared themselves to be on their side emotionally. Therefore, you need to use this character to not only build an emotional attachment between your reader and your protagonist, but also to use that attachment to manipulate the emotions of your reader. The protagonist is the character that you are going to leverage in order to get your reader nervous, curious, excited, happy, sad, angry, and any other emotion you want them to engage in throughout the experience. The best way to do that is to have a well-developed character that your reader can truly feel as though they have befriended.

Chapter 5: Additional Story Structure Tips

In addition to tips on basic story structure, developing a strong story, and how to create suspense, there are many other great tips that can help you when it comes to story structures. Now that you have the three important elements down, you can explore additional tips that will take you further into the realm of pro writer and help you generate a story that is going to be fantastic. The following tips are provided from real authors who have experience in writing their own high quality fiction materials. By following these tips, you can ensure that you don't only have a great story structure, but a phenomenal one.

Research Different Story Structures

Although there is a basic system that virtually all structures follow, it is important to understand that there are many modifications and alterations made to this structure in true writing. After all, if every story followed the basic structure down to the last detail then there would be no point in reading. We would be able to read the first chapter and know exactly how a book was going to turn out. By making modifications to the structure and playing it around in different ways, writers have the ability to stick to a structure that works while also providing a script that is unique, unpredictable, and engaging for readers.

Armed with this knowledge, you can prepare yourself to start researching many different story structures. The best way is to read other people's novels and do your best to identify the structure within' them. As you are reading, write down the major plot points and other key details that come into play with these plot points. Doing this will help you identify a series of structures that are used to create incredible novels, and how the writers spun them to work for the story. Do this several times over and pay attention to patterns that arise. Then, choose the structure you like most and make it work for your novel!

Stick to Structures that Are Traditional for Your Genre

For the best results, it is important that you stick to structures that are traditional to your genre. Although this may sound like a surefire way to create a story that sounds like every other story in the genre, it actually isn't. You will learn more about why in a moment. In the meantime, it is important that you understand why it is a good idea to stick to these traditional structures.

Each structure is designed to create a different effect for the story. Some build suspense, some build mystery, and some build both. Depending on what genre you are writing for, you are going to want to go for a structure that provides you with the right elements of virtually everything. These are going to be elements of suspense, story building opportunities, character development opportunities, and more. Each genre tends to be told in a unique way because it achieves a specific result. Therefore, each structure that is unique to each genre is built to help achieve that specific result. For example, you wouldn't want to use a suspense structure for a mystery novel because you would thus be identifying the perpetrator immediately. Likewise, you wouldn't want to use a mystery structure in a suspense novel because it would destroy the element of suspense by not giving enough information to the reader.

It is important that you do not reinvent the wheel, but rather you explore the different styles of wheels that exist for your market. Furthermore, just because you are limited to only using structures that are traditional for your genre does not mean that there is only one single structure you can follow. Each genre has its own selection of structures that will and won't work. The best way to identify which one you want to use is to read them, as described in the previous section, and pay attention to each type of structure you come across. As you do, identify which one would work best for your unique story and enlist that as your structure of choice.

Structure the Novel to Your Central Theme

As you are designing the structure for your novel, make sure that you are conforming the structure to fit the central theme of your novel and not the other way around. You never want to be derailing or detracting from the story as an attempt to stick to your structure. Remember, a structure is supposed to be a guideline that gets you to where you need to go. You do not have to follow it down to every last detail in order for your story to be a good one. Instead, you want to pay attention to the story structure and write your novel with that structure in mind.

Stories that are written to strictly to the guidelines set out in the structure end up sounding very forced and uncomfortable. Readers will often lose engagement quickly because the story becomes predictable and unnatural. They cannot relate to the story so they do not want to read it any longer. Ultimately, it takes away from the reader's experiences and kills the chance of your novel being greater.

To elaborate on how the structure *should* be used, we will explore how exactly you can enforce its guidelines. One of the biggest things you want to pay attention to, and use your structure for, is to ensure that your book stays focused on the central theme. If your novel strays too far away from the central theme at any given point, it may take away from the story overall. You never want to over share or get off track on a topic that does not contribute to the central theme or purpose of your novel. This is where your story structure comes in handy. Having a structure that can help keep you on track is highly valuable as it ensures that you do not derail your story and end up with a novel about love that gets too off track and ends up being about one person's career, or something else. Essentially you want to employ your story structure as a guide to keep you on track and to build a strong story, but you do not want to follow it so closely that you snuff out the quality of your story and produce something generic and predictable.

Modify the Template to Suit Your Plot

To expand further on the previous tip, it is important to work on modifying your template to suit your plot. Although you do not want to create an entirely new structure for your novel, or take one from the wrong genre, this does not mean that you cannot modify the template. For example, if you would prefer a certain plot point to happen sooner rather than later, or vice versa, you certainly have creative freedom to make this decision. Remember, you are a storyteller and your story is your work of art. Just because there are certain methods to use doesn't mean you can't get creative. For example, paint brushes are what you are *supposed* to paint with, but many choose to paint with sponges or even rags instead. Some even use a different material altogether, and yet the art is still incredible beautiful. In fact, it may be even more beautiful because of the unique method used. In this analogy, a different approach was used but the same bare basic structure was used: a tool was used to pick up paint and apply it to a canvas. You can easily modify certain parts of that, such as by changing your tools or picking a unique canvas, but at the very root is the same structure. The same goes for writing.

Just because authors before you have always used a specific template doesn't mean you cannot modify that template to suit your story. If you find that certain elements would serve better at a different area in the story, you are always welcome to do that. The best thing you can do as a writer is exercise your creative freedom. When you let loose from expectations and open yourself up to generate phenomenal content, inevitably you generate phenomenal content. As long as you stick to the bare bones basics with your structure, you are going to end up with a great story. If on the off chance you don't, it is a great opportunity to further research the structure and understand where you went wrong and how you could create a better story and structure in the future.

Create the Structure First, Modify it Later

It is always a good idea to begin your story with a strong structure. That being said, you should seek to create the structure before you begin writing. Having your structure created first and then creating a story around that structure helps ensure that you are staying on track with the basics. However, that does not mean that you are restricted to only writing to that specific structure.

As writers carry along the process of writing, they often find that it takes them down a natural path and therefore certain elements of their original structure no longer serve the story as powerfully as they could. The best thing to do in this circumstances is to reevaluate the structure and modify it so that it better suits the story in the direction that you have taken it. When you do this, you open yourself up to the opportunity of creating something much more powerful than you originally set out to do.

Creating a story is not always as straightforward as it seems. In many cases you will go into it with a very specific idea of what you want the story to be like and as a result of your writing process you discover that it actually works for reasons other than you thought so it naturally evolves away from your initial intentions. The best thing you can do in these circumstances is honor that natural evolution in your story and work with it. If you try and go against it in order to stick to your original structure you may end up creating a strange and unnatural twist backward, or it will otherwise not flow well. In order to give yourself creative freedom while also holding on to some sense of direction, the best thing to do is to start with a structure and modify it if your story evolves away from the initial structure you laid out for it. This will keep you on track while also giving you the potential to create an incredible story.

Hide the Structure in Your Writing

When it comes to the writing process, you want to ensure that you are hiding the structure within' your writing. It should not be painfully obvious what structure you have used. If it is, then your story will become predictable and people will lose interest. Virtually every story structure has been used several times over. This means that people will have a pretty easy ability to link your strategies together and determine what the novel will end like regardless of whether or not they have read it. They will also likely discover what major plot points are going to occur well before they ever happen. When the book becomes this predictable, it also becomes highly uninteresting.

A great writer knows how to hide the structure within' the story. Make things happen sooner or later than expected, twist away from the structure here and there to blend it in, and do your best to avoid going very clearly from point one to point two. You want your readers to question what is happening and be surprised along the way. Give them the idea that they have already arrived at the major plot point with one activity and then blow them out of the water with something much bigger. Keep the element of surprise active and use it as your weapon to bury the structure. The less obvious your structure is, the more unpredictable your story becomes and therefore the more power you have as the author to keep your reader engaged and have them wanting to learn more about what you have yet to tell them.

Keep Your Structure Organized and Handy

For a practical writing tip in regards to your structure, it is important that you keep it organized and that it is available at all times when you are writing. Your structure will prove to be a highly valuable tool when it comes to producing your novel. Being able to refer back to it at different points and identify where you are at will help you know where to go with your story, as well as help you stay focused on the central theme and overall purpose of your book.

A great way to keep your structure handy and useful during the writing process is to have it written down somewhere, such as on cue cards, and nearby whenever you are writing. This way you can identify where you have already been on the structure and where you have yet to go. It will also provide you with the ability to refer back to it regularly, as well as effortlessly revise it as needed. The reason why you might want to make your "final" structure on cue cards is because if you choose to modify it along the way you can easily do it without having to completely start over or rewrite it. This makes it effortless for you to modify it as needed and keep the parts you want.

Experiment

There is nothing more valuable than hands-on practice when it comes to any hobby, and this fact is not lost on writing. If you are looking for an opportunity to create an incredible book, take any chance you have to experiment. There are many ways that you can experiment when it comes to writing, and each can help you increase your understanding of story structures and how they work into the overall book, as well as how you can use your unique writing style to make the most of your story structure.

One great method is to take note of a few different story structures that will work effectively for the genre you are writing in and then draft your story out based on these. This means that you want to write a few paragraphs on each part of the structure and then read them together. It will give you the opportunity to see how your story would work together and if you have generated a strong enough story structure for your book. Another method is to practice writing short stories with different structures in a smaller way. While you won't be able to pack as much into the story as you would with a novel, it will give you a better idea of how your novel would sound with each unique structure in place.

Experimentation is the best way to practice writing and get an idea for what you like and what you don't like. If you are serious about it and you have time, practicing writing each novel with different structures and employing different strategies is a great way to see each structure in action and get a feel for how it works for your books. You can identify how the structure serves your story and where it might be weak, as well as how you can embed the structure within' the story using unique writing strategies to hide it from plain sight. This is a great way to practice writing overall and increase your skill if you are interested and have the time to invest.

Take Notes

Finally, a great method to use when it comes to learning and growing as a writer or as virtually anything is to take notes. When you are reading other books, take notes on what you like and don't like about the book, particularly when it comes to the structure of the book. When you are writing your own books, pay attention to where you have struggled and where you are succeeding. On the points where you a struggling, explore ways that you could make it easier. When it comes to each unique structure, write down how it serves your story and any thoughts you might have about how it could be better next time, or when you go through the editing process.

Taking notes allows you to review what you have already thought and felt about certain experiences with your story and its structure and gives you something easy and finite to look back on. When you take notes it means that you are not going to forget about or lose your thoughts in the process. This means that you can hold onto them and make the necessary changes without having to attempt to remember what it was that you wanted to do in the first place.

There are many great strategies you can use to strengthen your story structure immediately, as well as to help you increase your skills and become a better story writer through your structure over time. The more you emphasize on learning this skill now, the greater you will be at is as you go on. Remember that a strong structure can truly make or break a story. A bad structure equals a bad story, a good one equals a good story and a great structure will return you a great story. If you want to be great, you have to practice being great from the start. Over time and with practice you will graduate from being great to being phenomenal!

Conclusion

Thank you for reading *"Story Structure: Step-by-Step | Essential Story Building, Story Development and Suspense Writing Tricks Any Writer Can Learn"*. This book was designed to assist you in learning everything you need to know about story structures, including how you can make an incredible one.

I hope this book was able to elaborate on the concept of story structures, including what they are and why they are important. I also hope that you were able to learn plenty about how you can create your own story structure, develop your story, create suspense, and ultimately strengthen the structure of your story in order to create a phenomenal book.

The next step is to build your story structure and use it alongside the creation of your new book. Take your time and follow the steps within' this book to ensure that you have a strong structure that will serve you in the process of creating your book. Remember, as you go about the writing process you will want to check back to your structure to ensure that you are sticking to your original plan. However, if you find that your structure is no longer serving the overall creation of your story, you can always modify your structure for stronger impact. Sometimes the writing process can alter our plans and take us down a separate natural path. If this happens, ensure that you use the structure to support your story and the other way around.

Thank you!

CHARACTER DEVELOPMENT

STEP-BY-STEP

ESSENTIAL STORY CHARACTER CREATION, CHARACTER
EXPRESSION AND CHARACTER BUILDING
TRICKS ANY WRITER CAN LEARN

BOOK 3: CHARACTER DEVELOPMENT

STEP-BY-STEP

Essential Story Character Creation, Character Expression and Character Building Tricks Any Writer Can Learn

Sandy Marsh

reparation, damages, or monetary loss due to the information herein, either directly or indirectly.

Respective authors own all copyrights not held by the publisher.

The information herein is offered for informational purposes solely, and is universal as so. The presentation of the information is without contract or any type of guarantee assurance.

The trademarks that are used are without any consent, and the publication of the trademark is without permission or backing by the trademark owner. All trademarks and brands within this book are for clarifying purposes only and are the owned by the owners themselves, not affiliated with this document.

Table of Contents

Introduction

Thank you and congratulations for purchasing *"Character Development: Step-by-Step | Essential Story Character Creation, Character Expression and Character Building Tricks Any Writer Can Learn"*.

This book will help you with every aspect of character building, from creating the basic structure for your character to designing their personality and even helping develop them alongside the development of your story. Everything you will learn within' this book will ensure that you are equipped with all of the knowledge you need in order to create characters that are compelling and that your readers can fall in love with.

If you have read the previous five books from this series, then you will know just how important your characters are to your story. This guidebook will provide you with all of the knowledge you need in order to help create strong characters that will move your story forward and assist you in building the powerful and important emotional attachment between your reader and your characters.

Each chapter within' this book will provide you with part of the character building process. Within' that part you will be given step-by-step instructions so that you can easily create the best characters possible, knowing that they have been designed with every necessary feature to make them powerful additions and tools for your storytelling process. Without further ado, feel free to dive on into the character building experience. Enjoy!

Chapter 1: The Basics

It is no secret how important characters are to your story. They are the individuals that the story is about. Therefore, they are responsible for the story itself. They help you create the story, move the story forward, and introduce change and other action along the way. Without characters, there would be virtually no way for you to design a story.

Before we explore how you can build your own characters, we are going to explore the basics and important features of characters. This will help you understand more about why characters are so important and why you need them. It will also give you a foundational understanding of each unique style of character and how they can serve your story overall.

Why Characters Are Important

Stories are essentially created through verbal or written recollections of events that took place. In literary work, thoughts, choices, words, consequences, and actions are all important elements that are responsible for contributing to the plot line. Naturally, these qualities must be expressed in some form or manner. Since these are human qualities, it makes sense then that they would be expressed through a human-based character. Alternatively, such as in children's stories, they may be expressed through animal characters that possess these human-like qualities.

Characters are an important tool used by authors and writers to move stories forward. These are the personalities that give them the power to add the element of thought, action, words, choices, and consequences into their book. Without characters, they would essentially be describing a scene whereby nothing would be happening because there would be no one for it to happen to, for, or as a result of.

In order to establish themselves as useful tools that are used to move a plot forward, characters can be broken down into twelve categories. You will learn more about each of these categories in the next section. However, it is important to understand that each of these categories was designed to help create powerful and useable tools that writers can call on to help them progress the story forward.

Types of Characters

When you read a novel, you may be surprised to know that characters go a lot deeper than you think. In the novel, you watch the characters evolve, and new ones come and go along the way, but you may not understand how much actually goes into the development of these characters. When authors want to create a story that has a great deal of depth and can easily be believed as a real-life person, it is important that they understand the different types of characters that exist and how they can serve their story.

Naturally, fiction characters are made up. While they may be completely based on real people or have certain features borrowed from people that the author knows in real life, they are still made up characters. This is how the author is able to use them to build and move the story along because the characters can be used to achieve any outcome the author desires to create.

The following character styles will introduce you to twelve different types of characters that exist within' stories. By understanding each unique type of character, you can see how they can serve your story. Furthermore, you can decide what style each character will be designed in which will make it easier for you to discover the guidelines for creating the said character in the long run.

Major or Central Characters are characters that the story revolves around. These are the primary characters within' the story, and they are crucial to the development of the story itself. These are the characters who are presented with conflicts and who are responsible for executing the resolutions. Almost every part of the entire novel will revolve around these particular characters. They are often the main character, as well as that character's friends and family, or coworkers, or anyone else who will be used as a recurring character within' the story. These are some of the most important characters within' your novel because without them you will not have a story to tell. You want to emphasize your development on these characters to make sure that they are realistic, believable, and relatable to your readers.

Minor Characters are characters that are used to serve the major and central characters. These characters have a powerful role in helping to move the plot forward and often have as much depth as the major characters do. They are only considered minor characters, however, because they don't tend to recur as frequently as the major characters will and they are not a part of the central story. For example, they may be a sister that lives on another continent but comes to visit for a short time or even a few times for the duration of the novel. Alternatively, it may be a few coworkers that recur here and there but are not a part of the central theme or the majority of the major plot points. These are important characters because they help provide realistic depth to the book by broadening the scope of characters without taking complete attention away from the major characters themselves.

Dynamic Characters is a phrase used to represent characters that change over the course of the novel. Virtually anyone who changes his or her personality, belief system, morals or values, or even simply matures over the course of the novel is considered a dynamic character. These characters typically evolve for reasons primarily relating to the central theme of the book, such as the central conflict or a major crisis that they face that ultimately contributes to the books overall theme. Dynamic characters are not necessarily any one group of characters themselves. However, they can be virtually any character within' the book. The majority of the dynamic characters in a novel will typically be the major characters because these are the ones that are directly moving the story forward through change, as you learned about in previous books within' this book series. They may also turn out to be any other character within' the book, however. So long as a character changes in some noticeable way from the beginning to the end of the book they are considered a dynamic character.

Static Characters are the exact opposite of dynamic characters. These ones do not change over the course of the story. Instead, they remain the same. Completely unchanged. Static characters are not suitable to be major characters because they do not help progress a story or serve in the way of creating change in any way, shape, or form. Instead, static characters are usually minor characters. These characters still provide the author with the opportunity to use them as tools to spark change in the main characters, but they are not always required to change in order for the successful progression of the story.

Round Characters are unlike dynamic characters and unlike static characters altogether. These characters are ones that feature highly complex personalities. They may experience frequent conflicts, or they may even contradict themselves on a regular basis. These characters are also rarely used as major characters because the required personality type does not serve as a powerful foundation to generate a dynamic and moving character.

Flat Characters, unlike rounded characters, flat characters are typically notable for one single personality trait. This characteristic is one that should be the primary defining factor, influence, and expression that is used by the character. When you are creating a flat character, they are often much like a static character. And, similar to static characters, they are not suitable for the central characters because this personality does not provide the author with the opportunity to generate a moving enough character that will lead someone through a plot line.

Stock Characters are considered to be stereotypical characters that are almost expected in certain stories. For example, a cynical but moral private eye, mad scientists, and faithful sidekicks are all stock characters. These are all people that you would expect to be present in certain books. They generate the name "stock character" because of repetitive use in certain story types and structures. These characters typically have flat personalities, but may also have rounded personalities in some cases. They are a great element to add to your story because they give the reader something that they can identify with and expect, as well as someone that helps them feel like they can better relate to the story. It is a great way to give your reader a point to engage with through providing them with a familiar presence.

Protagonist is the word used to describe the central character in your story. This is the primary character that the story follows. They are at the center of your central characters, and they provide the main storyline. Most people call this the "main character," and they are identified as the "most important role in the story" to most, although this is not entirely true. Although this person is the reason the story exists, they are not the only one responsible for moving the plot forward. Therefore they are not the most important role. Still, they are highly important. This character should be dynamic and well-developed, as this will be the one your reader is going to follow most. Although the protagonist may not be the most likable character, they are the one that should be used in order to command that the reader experiences emotions, particularly empathy, for them. This way they can be used to draw the story forward and keep the reader engaged along the way.

Antagonist is the word used to describe either a character or a situation that operates against the protagonist. This is the opposition and the oppressive force that is trying to stop or otherwise hinder the success of the protagonist. This is the obstacle the protagonist faces that they must find the strength, knowledge, and power to overcome if they are going to generate a successful happy-ending story. As mentioned in the beginning, the antagonist can be a character *or* a situation. It can also be both. Even if you are using a situation instead of a character for your antagonistic force, you still want to go through the effort of making it well-developed so that the reader can believe it and understand why it is such a threat to the protagonist and their stakes.

Anti-Hero is a word used to describe a character that presents itself in certain stories. This is usually the protagonist, and they are called the anti-hero because they possess many features that make them unlikeable. They may have questionable morals, negative behavioral traits, or other characteristics that are not typically admired by the average person. This person may be the kind of individual that your reader would never want to associate with or root for, but still, they are the center of the story, and they find themselves following them and feeling empathy for this character when certain events happen. Writing an anti-hero protagonist can be difficult, but if you can master it, it is a great practice to help you increase your ability to generate empathy and emotional attachments between readers and your characters.

Foil Characters are those who have personalities and characteristics that often clash with other central characters in the novel. These characters may be used to represent the antagonist or a supporting character. They are designed by creating a character who has qualities that contrast the protagonist's character, or another important character within' the storyline. This contrast may seem unimportant, but from a writer's perspective, it provides you with the opportunity to highlight certain characteristics about your protagonist or other central character by emphasizing the differences between them and the foil character.

Symbolic Characters are ones that are used to resemble major parts of society through one character. These characters may be any major or minor character within' your story, so long as the entire purpose of the character is to highlight a certain aspect of society through their actions, beliefs, and values.

How Characters Are Presented and Revealed

Presenting and revealing characters is your opportunity to teach your reader who the character is and what they're all about. This is where you get the ability to introduce them to different characteristics and traits that the reader should know about the character, and how these traits contribute to the way that the character ties into the storyline.

There are only two ways that you can present your characters to your readers: either through direct or indirect presentation.

Direct presentation is the method you use when you are directly telling your readers about who the character is. For example, if you were to write "Presenting to you, Christopher Adams, a self-righteous, ignorant, and exploitative agent who preys on his clients for their money." In this circumstance, you are directly telling your reader who Christopher Adams is and what his most outstanding traits are. You can also do it in a more positive light, such as "Meet Mary Willows, a school teacher who spends her time eating peanut butter sandwiches and teaching preschoolers how to count to five. She is always bright and cheery, and will put a smile on your face faster than even a puppy could." In essence, direct presentation is described as any type of presentation you make whereby you tell the reader what they need to know.

Indirection Presentation is naturally the exact opposite of direct presentation. This is the tactic you use when you leave it up to the reader to get to know a character through his or her words, thoughts, and actions. They get to know this person through what they say and do throughout the book, allowing them to generate their own theories on who this character is. Still, you use their words and actions to help you create the overall illusion as to what makes the character who they are. This form of presentation is very similar to the natural way that we get to know people since we are not given direct answers when we meet people.

Instead, we have to learn about them based on what they say and do. Unlike direct presentation, indirect presentation is the tactic used when authors allow readers to formulate judgments and opinions on characters without ever telling them about the quality traits these characters have. Sometimes the reader will know exactly who the character is and their judgment is right, and other times they will be proven wrong over the course of the book.

To make it easier for you to use these two presentation methods to introduce who your characters are, we have compiled a list of the eleven basic ways that you can present your characters to your readers. This list is compiled to provide examples of both direct and indirect presentation methods. You can also use it as a test to see if you can determine which would be considered direct and which would be considered indirect so that you can better understand how both of these presentation styles work.

1. Present your character by having them say things in a particular way.

2. Present your character by having them say certain things.

3. Present your character by providing insight into their environment.

4. Present your character by exploring what they think.

5. Present your character by providing a physical description of them.

6. Present your character by providing a psychological description of them.

7. Present your character by telling readers what other people say or think about them.

8. Present your character by having them do certain things.

9. Present your character by having them do things in a particular way.

10. Present your character by the way that they react to other's actions and words.

11. Present your character by the way that they react to their own actions and words.

Chapter 2: What Makes a Character Great

Since you are researching how to make the characters for your novel, let's assume that you don't just want to make a good character. Instead, you want to make a great character. You want to make the kind of character that people are eager to read more about. This character is one that the reader can somehow attach to. It also gives you the best tool to help you move your story forward, regardless of what type of character you are creating. Some of these techniques should be used on all characters while others only need to be used on a few, which you will learn about as you read on. Still, every character in your novel is important to the storyline itself. Therefore, they all need to be great characters. This chapter will help you identify exactly what is required in order for you to be able to do just that.

Have Characters that Are Likeable

While not all of your characters have to be likable, many should be. Your protagonist, for example, should be a likable character unless you are spinning them off as an anti-hero. Having likable characters in your book will make people have an easier ability to emotionally connect to your characters. Just as you would prefer to spend time with and invest your energy in people you like in real life when people read they also like to invest their energy and attention into characters that they like. At least a few of your characters should be likable so that your reader feels as though they can relate to the character and generate some form of emotional attachment and relationship with that character as they read your story.

As you are creating likable characters, however, avoid making them saint-like. You do not want to have a character that is *too* likable or features little to no flaws because this actually goes back in the opposite direction. It takes away from the realistic values of your character and makes them seem unapproachable, which, ironically makes them unlikeable. So, avoid trying to make your characters *too* likable, or people won't like them! Instead, create a realistic character who has believable flaws that are enough to balance out their likable qualities so that they are still likeable while also being realistic and relatable.

Have Characters that Are Not Likeable

In addition to having characters that are likable, you need to have ones that aren't! Any real-life story would include people who are not liked by the protagonist, and who may be unlikeable in general. These are the ones whose flaws outweigh their good traits. They are still human, therefore they still naturally have some good qualities to them, but overall they are not likable as a person. In a typical story, this is your antagonist, but it doesn't always have to be. Furthermore, you can have more people who are unlikeable, such as someone who is related to or close to the protagonist. Using unlikeable characters helps to balance out the number of likable characters you have, thus making the story sound more relatable and realistic.

Again, you don't want to create a character that is *too* unlikeable, or people aren't going to believe it. Typically, even the worst people have some positive characteristics to them that make them worth having empathy for, even if we don't tend to like them in general. Make sure that you keep your unlikeable character's human by giving them some characteristics that make them seem as though they *could* be likable in some way or another, even if only a little.

Make Your Characters Good at What They Do

Even though your characters, particularly your protagonist, should face difficulties and come to the end of their rope once or twice before finally succeeding, they should still succeed in the end. Furthermore, they should be good at what they do, even if it isn't always enough to get them to a full success. For example, they should be a phenomenal secret agent that is exposed to acts of god that make it impossible for them to capture the bad guy until *finally* things go right and they succeed at last. Even if they make mistakes from time to time or they struggle to be the best here and there, they should typically be good at what they do. If they aren't, people are going to wonder why they are even trying to begin with and it will make the story unlikeable.

Think about stories such as the James Bond ones. If James Bond were to fail every mission he ever set out to accomplish it would not make for a good story. People may laugh their way through one show, but it would not last, and they certainly wouldn't have many different movies based on this hero. Likewise, your heroic character should be good at what they do, and they should be worthy of your reader cheering them on for the duration of your story.

Give Your Characters a Strong Charisma

Having characters that are charismatic increases their likeability. It doesn't only draw in other characters, but it draws in the reader as well. While charisma as far as good looks can be a beneficial factor, this is more about their qualities. Make them someone who lights up the room when they walk in it. Maybe they are particularly happy, or they always have a good joke to share. Or, maybe they are great at complimenting others and making them feel good about themselves. Whatever way you choose to build charisma in the character, make sure you take the time to actually establish it. Remember, you want likable characters and charisma is one great way to create a character that can be liked. The more drawn into the character your reader is, the more invested they will become in your story overall.

Have Dynamic Characters

Characters that love to take driven action and grow alongside your plot line are great when it comes to building a strong book. As you know, it is good to have your protagonist as a dynamic character. However, you should consider adding a few other dynamic characters as well. Having the antagonistic character, as well as supporters of both the protagonist and antagonist being designed to be dynamic characters means that you have plenty of opportunities to pursue action in your story. It also makes the story much more relatable and realistic.

When you are creating dynamic characters, know that not every character in the story needs to be dynamic. In fact, it is better to have a strong balance between dynamic and static characters. Remember, in real life, we have a little bit of everything. If you can look at your own life, there are likely people who have never changed or haven't been in your own life story enough for their change to be recognized, and then there are those who have grown drastically since you met them. Just like in real life, your book needs to have a healthy mixture of both as well. This will ensure that your reader feels as though your story is compelling and enjoyable.

Let Your Characters Suffer

Some of the novels are going to require your characters to suffer. Conflicts, complex issues, and various situations would lead to any normal person facing the experience of suffering in their own life. The same goes for your characters. If someone dies, let the character suffer. Allow them to feel the suffering. If they lose something, something doesn't go their way, or they are otherwise facing challenges, allow them to experience some suffering alongside those challenges. This makes them more believable and relatable. Furthermore, it draws your reader's emotions into the story even more. Letting your character suffer somewhat is a great way to build empathy from your reader to your character. Once your reader has empathy, they are much more likely to care about what's next for your character. They want to see the character do well and they are eager to see them win, so the reader roots even more for your character. You can build on this throughout the story by introducing a few different instances of suffering. Just, as with everything, make sure you don't go overboard and have too much suffering, or the book will be too depressing and unbelievable to read!

Know Your Character Intimately

It is important that you know your character intimately. Even more intimately than your readers ever will, even though they need to get to know them intimately as well. When you know your characters intimately, you can easily talk about them, share their story, and give insight into their inner world. This is because you would know how they would think, speak, act, and react in various situations. You also know their preferences, dislikes, likes, and other important characteristics about them.

Think about someone that you know well. You have likely known someone at one point or another in your life so well that you know exactly what they would do or say in most situations. This is how intimately you need to know your characters, as this is the intimacy that will allow you to write about them in any and every situation that will arise throughout your novel. You should know exactly how that person would respond to everything you throw their way so that you can create a realistic and believable character. This is what takes your character from a profile on paper to a real person in your fiction novel.

Chapter 3: Character Building Step-by-Step

Now that you are clear on why characters are important, the basics about characters, and what makes a character great instead of just good, you are ready to start actually building your characters. As you go through this chapter, keep what you have already learned in mind as it will help you stay focused and create successful characters along the way.

In this chapter, you are going to discover step-by-step guidance for picking whom you want to cast in your book, as well as how you can develop each character so that they serve your book in a powerful and profound way. Depending on what type of character you are working towards developing, you will discover a guide to help you develop that kind of character. This will ensure that each character is developed enough to be useful in your novel, but that you aren't wasting your time over-developing characters that do not require it, such as minor static characters.

Choosing Your Cast

Before you begin developing your characters you need to decide which characters you want to cast in your book. That is, you need to decide how many characters you are going to need to actually write the book. While you may find that some additional ones come up or you feel naturally called to pull in new characters along the way, you should start out with a pretty strong idea as to whom your central, minor, and other characters are going to be from the beginning. Anyone who is going to be essential to your central story should be outlined and developed before you begin writing. This will ensure that you know exactly how and when to present them, and their presentation is natural and strong based on their unique character and role in the novel.

The best way to choose how many characters you need for your novel is to refer back to your story structure and outline. Looking at your story structure and outline will give you the opportunity to consider each major plot point. As you do, consider which characters should be present for the plot point, as well as which ones are necessary for it. Take your time and work your way through the plot, picking out characters as you go. Once you have, take a look at the "in between" parts, too. For example, in between major plot points, you may need additional characters to keep the story flowing, such as people in line at a bank or the cashier at the local grocer. This is the best way to determine what characters you need in your novel and will have you well on your way to a strong character roster.

Once you have determined which characters are needed for the plot, you want to get more specific about them. First, make sure that you haven't picked too many characters. A book with too many characters can be overwhelming and can lead to your reader forgetting who is who. However, you want to make sure that you have enough that you can make it feel like real life. The best way to make sure you have enough characters, and not too few or too many, is to make sure that every single character you choose to create is essential to the story itself. Then, you need to decide what kind of character they're going to be. Are they going to be a major character or a minor character? Additionally, will they be round, flat, static, or dynamic? Pay attention to these features as they will help you determine how to create them.

Creating Your Characters

Central characters are the main characters in your novel. They include the protagonist, the antagonist, and any other characters that are regularly involved in the plot, including major plot scenes. When you are creating central characters, you want to go heavily into depth about who they are and why they are that way. Below you will find several categories filled with questions. Answering these questions will help you answer about who your character is, which will help you develop them and learn a great deal of information about them. This way you can get to know them intimately and write about them effortlessly.

Character's General Information

1. What is your character's name?

2. Do they have a nickname? If so, what is the story behind it and who gave it to them?

3. Do they like their nickname?

4. What is their birthday?

5. Where were they born?

6. What ethnicity are they?

7. Do they have any religious views?

8. Do they practice their religion?

9. Where do they currently live? (Be specific with their address)

10. Do they rent the place or own it?

11. Briefly describe their home.

12. Does anyone else live with them?

13. What is it like where they live? (i.e., city, town, etc.)

14. Do they like living here? If not, why not? Where would they rather be?

15. What type of home décor do they have? (i.e., expensive, neat, inexpensive, comfortable, etc.)

16. What is the first impression someone would have to their home?

17. Do they have pets? If not, why not? If they do, what
kind, what are their names, and how many? How do
they treat their pets?

18. What job do they presently have, how long have
they had it for, and where is their job located?

19. Do they like their job?

20. How much money do they make?

21. What educational background do they have?

22. Do they drive? If so, what kind of vehicle do they
have? Be specific.

23. What is their sexuality?

24. Are they in a romantic relationship with anyone? If
so, who and for how long?

25. Do they have any previous romantic partners that are
significant to the story?

26. What do they call their current spouse? (i.e.,
nicknames)

27. How did they meet their spouse?

28. Do they have any children? Give specific details if they do. (i.e., age, birthday, gender, name, who the parents are, etc.)

29. If they have children, describe the relationship they share with each child.

Physical Appearance

1. How tall is this character?

2. What do they weigh?

3. What body type do they have? (i.e., skinny, curvy, overweight, athletic, etc.)

4. What color are their eyes?

5. Do they use glasses, contacts, or hearing aids? Or any other medical devices?

6. What is their skin tone?

7. Do they have any prominent features that one might notice about them? (i.e., freckles, birthmark, scar, tattoos, etc.)

8. What is their face shape?

9. Whom do they look similar to?

10. What is their overall health like?

11. Do they have any chronic illnesses or conditions?

12. Are there any current health problems they are facing?

13. How do they dress? (Including cost range of clothes and specific style)

14. Do they dress to be noticed, or just to be dressed?

15. Do they wear any special or significant pieces of jewelry or accessories?

16. How does this character approach their grooming habits? (i.e., extremely neat, unkempt, etc.) Why do they groom themselves this way?

17. What hairstyle does this character have?

18. What is the natural hair texture for this character?

19. If they typically groom their hair for a different texture, what is it?

20. What is their natural hair color?

21. If they dye their hair, what color is it now?

Communication

1. When communicating, what is the pace that this person communicates with? (i.e., fast, slow, average)

2. What tone of voice do they have?

3. Do they have any words they tend to use or favor in general conversation?

4. What are their vocabulary patterns? (I.e., educated, precise, vulgar, etc.)

5. What is their demeanor when communicating? (I.e., cool and confident, nervous, etc.)

6. What posture do they tend to have?

7. Do they use gestures frequently in communication? If so, how often?

8. What are their common body language gestures or signals? (i.e., nail-biting, clenching fists, shoving hands in pockets, etc.)

Daily Behaviors & Habits

1. How does this character manage their finances? (i.e., saves a lot, living paycheck to paycheck, etc.)

2. Do they acquire any of their finances illegally? If so, how?

3. Do they have any personal habits that may be based on addictions? (i.e., drinking, smoking, gambling, etc.)

4. What is their morning routine? Be specific.

5. What does their average day look like? Be specific.

6. Do they ever have lunch in any particular spot?

7. What is your character's dinner routine? Be specific.

8. What does your character do after dinner? Be specific.

9. What is your character's bedtime routine? Be specific.

10. Does your character have any skills or talents? If so, do they share them or are they hidden and/or kept private?

11. What is your character unskilled at, or bad at? How do they feel about these flaws?

12. Do they have any hobbies?

Character's Past

1. Where is your character's hometown?

2. What was their childhood like? Do they remember it?

3. What is their earliest memory?

4.   What is their saddest memory?

5.   What is their happiest memory?

6.   Did your character attend school? If so, how much?
     Did they enjoy school? Why or why not?

7.   What is the most significant event that took place in
     your character's childhood?

8.   Do they have any other significant childhood
     events?

9.   What past jobs have they had that are significant to
     them?

10. Do they have a criminal record?

11. If your character does have a criminal record, how
     did they get it and where were they when the event
     happened?

12. Did they get any convictions or sentences? Did they
     serve time?

13. Who was the first person that your character loved?

14. When was their first sexual experience? Do think
    look back on it as a positive memory or a negative
    one?

15. Has your character experienced any major accidents
    or traumas in their life? If so, are they still affected
    by them? How?

Family Tree

1. Who is your character's mother? What is her full name?

2. Is she alive or deceased?

3. What is or was the mother's occupation?

4. What is the relationship that your character shares with their mother?

5. Who is your character's father? What is his full name?

6. Is he alive or deceased?

7. What is or was the father's occupation?

8. What is the relationship that your character shares with their father?

9. Does the character have any additional parental figures, such as a step-parent, foster parents, adoptive parents, biological parents, or even an adult who was of parental influence in their life such as a close family friend?

10. If they were adopted, do they know about it?

11. Does your character have any siblings? If so, list
    them by age in birth order. Include their names and
    how they are related to the character. (i.e., full
    sibling, step-sibling, half-sibling, etc.)

12. What type of relationship does your character share
    with each of their siblings?

13. Does your character have any nieces or nephews? If
    so, what are the relationship(s) like?

14. Do they have any in-laws? If so, what are the
    relationship(s) like?

15. Who else is a part of the character's family that is
    significant to the story, aside from those already
    listed?

Relationships

1. Who is your character's best or closest friend? How long have they known each other and where did they meet?

2. Do they have any other close friends? If so, how long has your character known them and where did they meet?

3. How is your character perceived by their friends?

4. How is your character perceived by strangers?

5. How is your character perceived by their spouse or lover?

6. How is your character perceived by their past spouses/lovers?

7. How is your character perceived by their children, if they have any?

8. How is your character perceived by their other family members?

9. How is your character perceived by the opposite sex?

10. How is your character perceived by children in general?

11. How is your character perceived by others who have more success than them?

12. How is your character perceived by others who have less success than them?

13. How is your character perceived by their boss, if they have one?

14. How is your character perceived by their co-workers?

15. How is your character perceived by their competitors?

16. How is your character perceived by authorities? (i.e., police, doctors, attorneys, etc.)

17. How does your character react to people who challenge them?

18. How does your character react to people who anger them?

19. How does your character react to people who ask for help?

20. What do others tend to like most about your character?

21. What do they like least or consider to be the character's biggest flaw?

22. Does this character have any secret attractions to others? If so, have they been explored?

23. In romantic relationships, is your character typically faithful or unfaithful? If they are unfaithful, does their partner(s) know it?

24. What are they like during sexual encounters? (inhibited and shy or outgoing and wild?) Does this change over the course of the story or their life? If it does, why?

25. Who does your character like the least out of everyone in the story? Why?

26. Who does your character like the most out of everyone in the story? Why?

27. Who does your character consider to be the most important person in their life right now, and why do they feel this way?

28. Who is your character romantically attracted to at the moment, and why?

29. Who is your character's role model or idol? Why? And are they famous, or no?

30. Who does your character consider to be their enemy, if anyone?

31. Who does your character tend to misjudge or misunderstand the most?

32. Who tends to misunderstand or misjudge your character the most?

33. Is there anyone whom your character has lost touch within their lifetime who was significant to them? If so, why and how has it affected your character?

34. What was the worst ending to any relationship your character has had? (romantic or otherwise)

35. Who do they typically rely on when it comes to receiving advice?

36. Who does your character tend to rely on when it comes to emotional support?

37. Who does your character support, either emotionally or with advice, the most?

Attitude & Beliefs

1. Does your character have any psychological issues such as phobias, mental illnesses, or otherwise?

2. Do they tend to be optimistic or pessimistic?

3. Do you know the Meyer Briggs personality type for your character? (This can give a lot of information about how they would react and respond in a variety of situations.)

4. When is your character the most comfortable in life? (i.e., when drinking, when with certain people, when alone, etc.)

5. When are they the least comfortable? (i.e., when public speaking, in certain locations, around certain people, when drinking, etc.)

6. Does your character tend to be cautious, reckless, or brave in how they approach their life?

7. What does your character value and prioritize the most? (i.e., family, religion, friends, fun, money, success, etc.)

8. Who does your character love the best?

9. What or who would your character be willing to die for?

10. How does your character tend to be towards others? (i.e., compassionate, arrogant, selfish, sensitive, etc.)

11. What is the personal philosophy of your character?

12. What is your character most embarrassed about?

13. What is their greatest wish?

14. Do they have any prejudices against other people? If so, what and why?

15. What are their political beliefs?

16. Do they believe in any superstitions, fate, or destiny?

17. What is the greatest strength that your character possesses?

18. What is the greatest weakness that your character possesses?

19. What other positive or strong characteristics does your character possess?

20. What other negative or weak characteristics does your character possess?

21. What does your character favor most about their own attributes? (Both physical and personality-wise)

22. What does your character despise most about their own attributes? (Both physical and personality-wise)

23. Are these feelings accurate, or are they over or underplayed?

24. How does your character think other people perceive them? Is this accurate?

25. What does your character regret the most in life?

26. Do they have any other regrets?

27. What are the biggest secrets that your character has?

28. Does anyone else know about these secrets? If so, who?

29. How do they react in a crisis?

30. What tends to cause the most problems in their life? (i.e., finances, colleagues, friends, family, health, etc.)

31. How do they react to change?

32. Do they have any quirks?

33. What would your character like to change about themselves the most?

34. Give a short paragraph (100 words or less) of the character describing themselves to others.

35. What are their short-term goals?

36. What are their long-term goals?

37. Do they have any plans to achieve the goals, or do they believe they are out of reach?

38. How would others be affected by your character reaching these goals? Do this effects matter to your character?

39. If anything is stopping your character from achieving their goals, what is it?

40. What are they actively working to protect, keep, or gain right now?

41. What event or situation do they most fear or dread being in?

42. What person would your character want to be, if they could be anyone?

43. Who would they absolutely not want to be?

Likes & Favorites

1. What is your character's favorite food?

2. What is your character's favorite drink?

3. What color do they like most?

4. Do they have a favorite book?

5. Do they have a favorite film?

6. What song or music genre do they prefer?

7. Do they watch TV? If so, what do they watch?

8. Does your character have a favorite sport?

9. Does your character have a motto or a quote that they like?

10. Where do they like to hang out or spend most of their time?

11. What do they own that is their favorite possession?

This list may seem extremely exhausting, but trust that all of this information will help you get to know your character intimately. Once you have the answers to all of these questions, you will know your character so well that it will be effortless for you to write about them and their natural evolution over the course of your novel. Do your best to fill in the entire questionnaire so that you have plenty of material to write on and that nothing is left up to chance. A writer who has extremely strong characters is one who knows their characters so well that they could easily answer any of these questions about them. Keep your character profile handy so that you can refer back to it during the writing process as needed.

A Word on Minor Characters

Naturally, you don't need to have an elaborate profile for your minor characters. Instead, go through the list and pick the questions that you feel relate most to how the character fits into the story. For example, if it is a friend from high school that your protagonist sees once or twice during the entire book, you likely don't need to include much. You may want to fill out the general section, the past section, and the likes and favorites section. Even then, it may not be necessary for you to fill out the entire thing. When it comes to designing minor characters, use your judgment to create a character that has depth, without wasting your time developing a character further than you actually need to for the benefit of your overall book.

Chapter 4: Creating Expression

How your character expresses themselves is a really important part of how they contribute to the story itself. Their expression is ultimately how your character conveys themselves to others. This will be how they express their thoughts and opinions, and how they portray themselves to others to interpret them and who they are. You want to make sure that, just like with your character development, you develop how your character expresses themselves as well. While this part of the book will not go into as elaborate of a guide as the previous chapter did, we will explore various ways that you can create an expression for your character, as well as for all of the characters within' your book as a whole.

Catch Phrases

Having characters have their own catchphrases is a great way to build an expression in your character and give them a unique voice. This should be a catchphrase that only one character uses, even though other characters may sometimes paraphrase that character to be funny or to otherwise quote them. Still, it should be known that this phrase is unique to that specific character.

Don't overuse catch phrases in your book or it will take away from the value of them. Ideally, only one or *maybe* two characters should have a catch phrase in your book. Also, avoid it being the main character unless they are only going to use the catchphrase from time to time. The catch phrase is a great way to give foreshadowing effects, but with too many, it can take away and just sound cheesy or poorly written.

Group-Specific Slang Words

If you look at most friend groups in real life, they have their own way of speaking. This way of speaking often includes their own selection of slang words. If you want to increase the expression and voice of your overall group, as well as each character that is a part of it, seek to make slang words or group mottos that are used by everyone in the group. However, make sure that none of the slang or mottos are anywhere close to the one character's catchphrase or you will confuse the reader. Instead, simply choose expressions and terms that this group will speak in that others likely don't. This makes them unique and gives them a very realistic feel, since this is completely natural behavior in real life, too.

Other Worldly Slang

If you are writing a fantasy book that takes your characters to another world, consider using other worldly slang that you have made up in order to help set them apart. In a group, each person speaks differently from one another, just as how each individual in a country – or likely the entire world – speaks differently. You likely wouldn't go to a different planet and hear everyone speaking in typical American dialect. For that reason, it is a good idea to create and include other worldly phrases and slang that help the reader differentiate the characters.

Gender-Specific Phrases

If you ever pay attention to a real-life crowd, men and women tend to express themselves in extremely different ways. You can bring this type of gender-specific expression into your novel, too. And, in fact, you should. By including as many different unique elements of expression in your novel as you can, you make the novel more believable, and your readers have an easier time relating to it. While you don't have to use gender stereotypes to create the expressions between each gender, you should make it clear that they are two different genders speaking and expressing themselves. If you need inspiration, spend some time with a group of males and then spend some time with a group of females and you will see the differences. If you want to take it even further, afterward spend some time with a mixed group and you will still notice that each gender expresses themselves differently, even in front of the other sex.

Career and Industry Jargon

People in different careers and industries typically speak in unique tongues. They have industry and career-specific jargon that they use when they are talking to their colleagues. When you are building characters who have jobs, careers, or are heavily involved in certain industries, make sure that you include some jargon from that job, career, or industry in their vocabulary. In the real world, people would naturally pick up on and use this jargon. Therefore, your character should too.

Body Language

It is no secret that body language is a major part of how we communicate with others and express ourselves. Use body language in your book, too. If characters are feeling attacked or bullied and they are feeling particularly low or closed off, have them standing with a closed expression such as with their arms crossed and skulking away from the attacker. If the character is happy, have them standing tall and proud with their body casual but a bright smile on their face. Using body language as a means to help your characters communicate on an even more advanced level will help you when it comes to expressing your characters. While you don't need to explain their body language at every moment, a good idea is to introduce what they look like when they're feeling neutral and then only talk about their body language if it is vastly different from what it would be when they're in that neutral state. If you are unsure about what body language people would be using when they're talking or when they're feeling different things, consider briefly studying it. There are many online and print resources available that are made specifically to help people further understand body language. Knowing it more intimately may help you when it comes to helping your character express themselves.

Sometimes when you are creating certain scenes, body language can speak more to the reader and other characters than the communicating character's own words will. For example, if the character is lying to someone else, have their words telling a lie while their body exposes the truth about them lying. Maybe they are telling a lie, and in the meantime, they are sweating, and they have shoved their hands into their pockets. Body language can teach people a lot about what is truly going on in your character's mind, beyond what they say, so be sure to use it at the appropriate times for greater expression.

Dialect

Make sure your character's dialect is true to where they come from. If they are from the southern states, for example, have them use a southern dialect. You may even have presented their accent to the reader. If they are from somewhere else, such as a foreign country, use the dialect that is natural to where that person comes from. Using proper native dialect not only helps create a realistic element to your characters but it also helps you contrast between your characters if you have a few that are from different areas or countries.

Regional Slang

Most regions have their own slang that is unique from other regions. Just like their dialect differs from place to place, so too does their choice in slang words. In the majority of cases kids and teens are more likely to use slang over adults, so make sure that the younger demographic uses a lot more slang than the older demographic. Furthermore, ensure that the slang that your younger demographic is using is age specific and that your older demographic is using age-specific terms. The adults may occasionally use terms from the younger demographic, but don't make this happen often and make sure that you make it clear that they have borrowed it from someone in the younger generation.

General Vocabulary

In addition to all of the other steps in this chapter, make sure that you take a look at your character's vocabulary in general. Everyone tends to speak a certain way, often slightly different from other people. To put it bluntly, there are some people that just don't say some things because it's not a part of their standard vocabulary. The best thing to do is to get an idea of what your character's overall vocabulary is. Since vocabulary and the words, they could use go so far, the better idea is to outline what they don't say and would never say. This helps you get an idea for their style of communication and what they actually would say.

Creating expression takes time and practice, but if you follow these tips and have patience, you should be well on your way to creating strong terms of expression for all of your characters. Remember, when it comes to really planning out each character, don't worry too much about creating a very specific set of expressions for characters who have an extremely minor role in the story. Instead, focus on those who are minor but recurring, or those who are central characters. These are the ones who you really want to go into depth with when planning their expressions. Take your time and work through each of these steps while planning out how the character will express themselves in each one and use this as your opportunity to get to know your character even more. This will make it much simpler to know how your character will express themselves and communicate with others in your novel.

Chapter 5: Bringing Your Character to Life

Finally, you want to bring your character to life! This is the part of the process where you take that perfect profile you've made on paper, and you start bringing each character to life for the first time. This is where you get to turn them into real characters that will have prominent roles in your novel in one way or another. Through the following steps, you will tie up any loose ends and then ultimately unleash your character into the world. Once this part of the process is done, you can start writing your story, trusting that your characters will be strong enough to support the plot line and make your story truly great.

Use Inspiration from People You Actually Know

There is a good chance that the characters you have made somehow resemble someone you already know in real life. When we are creating characters, we are often drawn on inspiration from those that we already know. Don't feel shy when doing this! When you are writing, feel open to the idea of drawing on more inspiration for situations where you might need it. For example, if you are truly struggling to identify how your character would act, react, respond, or speak in any given situation, draw inspiration from that person! This will help their actions flow naturally so that they seem realistic to who the character truly is. It is never a bad thing to draw on this inspiration, so keep it handy and use it at your own discretion to help increase the quality of your story, simplify the writing process, and create a compelling character that fits perfectly into your story.

Play on the Element of Surprise

Sometimes readers expect a certain thing when they are reading. For example, if your characters are going into a night club your reader will likely expect that the bouncer is some big gangly guy who would easily knock anyone down who tried to slip through uninvited. Instead of simply going with the person that your reader would assume the character would look like, pick someone unique who makes your reader feel surprised towards who is playing the role. For example, you might pick a slender and somewhat lanky character who looks like they would struggle to keep a small dog back, let alone a potential customer who was serious about getting in. Instead of having a tall, white, male lawyer, consider having someone from a completely different demographic. Character's don't need to be exactly who you would assume they would be. In fact, they're often better when they aren't whom you expect them to be, yet this is still phenomenal at their role.

In addition to using the element of surprise in your characters, use it in your events, too. Don't be afraid to make the unexpected happen and keep your readers on their toes. Use events that they wouldn't have expected create settings that are unlike what they would have expected, and ultimately give your reader a reason to think "Oh, wow! Really?" This element of surprise is a great way to bring your characters and book itself to life. Most real-life experiences don't go as planned and often many unexpected events, people, and circumstances come to light in our lives. Do the same with your book, both with characters, events, and circumstances. You want your reader to feel like it is real life and that they never know what to expect from one day to another. This increases the value of your story and also heightens your reader's engagement and commitment towards your book.

Use Contradictions

Strong characters often have qualities that are highly contradictory. People aren't always as they seem, and so your character's shouldn't be as well. A great way to increase the livelihood of your characters and bring them to life is to give them contradictions. For example, an incredibly sporty race car driver who is obsessed with the opera. Using these contradictions in your characters remind people that they're human and that they aren't always logical box-fitting characters. Instead, they are real, and they have interesting quirks about them just like we all do.

Give Your Characters Goals

In the character developing chapter we explored the goals that your character has, but now we really want to emphasize on that. Giving your character's goals, hopes, dreams, and fantasies about how they want the future to be for themselves make them a lot more life-like. Real life people always have some form of goal or dream, whether they talk about it or not. Giving your characters these features is important because it gives them something to look forward to, and something for your reader to look forward to with them. It gives your reader a deeper insight into your character's inner world and what makes them tick, therefore making your reader feel a lot more connected to your character.

Discover Their Image

Through the character development process, we discovered many identifying factors that shed light on what your character's actual image was, but if you really want to make them life-like, you want to discover exactly what it is like. One great way to do this is to find a picture of someone on Google or otherwise who represents your character. They should look similar both in physical appearances and in the way they present themselves through style and expression. Many great writers claim that they will even print these pictures off and keep them nearby so that they can truly look at their characters and gain insight from them during the writing process, to help progress the story along. If this feels right for you, certainly go ahead and borrow this tip from other writers.

One thing to note about your character's image is that despite you know it intimately, you don't want to over explain it to your readers. Instead, give away important pieces of information but let your reader develop a picture in their own mind. When your reader generates their own image of who your character is and what they look like it becomes more engaging and more personal. Then, your reader is more likely to connect with your character and feel a form of emotional attachment towards them.

Listen to Them

Many writers claim that they can actually *hear* their character's voices. They start often by hearing a voice on the television or somewhere in public that sounds extremely similar to their character's own voice. Then, they listen to that person and try to generate a total voice from it. Through that, they are able to listen to the voice of the character and use that to help them move forward.

Each character has their own unique voice. This is a combination of how they speak, what they are saying, and all of the tone and emotion that goes into their words. You want to discover the voice of each of your characters when you are writing because this makes the sense of expression and speaking for them much easier. This is where you get the opportunity to bring them to life because they become a voice that, eventually, everybody hears somewhere. They may also hear it through someone on television or in public, but ultimately they can relate it back and go "hey that sounds like so and so from that book I just read!" When this happens, you have truly made your character life-like to the highest degree.

Practice

It may take some time, but as with all things, you need to practice. Practicing bringing your characters to life and making them realistic is a great way to truly discover how you can do it to the highest of your abilities. At first, it may feel uncomfortable or even unnatural, but quickly you will find an opportunity to make your characters even more life-like, and it will all just flow together.

One great way to practice is to consider an everyday situation. It doesn't have to be one that is going to be involved in your book, just consider an everyday situation, such as going into a coffee shop and talking to the barista. Then, write a few paragraphs for each character that you are trying to bring to life. Consider how they would walk into the café, how they would communicate with the barista, where they would go to stand after they've ordered, how they would carry their coffees, whether they would drink the coffee there or go elsewhere. Consider whether they have someone with them or if they're alone. How do they express themselves to other patrons in the coffee shop? Get very specific about how their visit would go through these paragraphs. This is a great way to really consider how your character would react in everyday situations, thus making it a lot easier for you to get to know your own character personally. Remember, once you know them intimately it becomes a lot easier to share them with your readers.

Give Your Characters Plenty of Opportunities to Show Up

Giving your character the opportunity to show the reader how they react in different situations is a great way to bring them to life. Put your characters into many different situations and give your reader the opportunity to see them in action in every single one. Share about how your character acts in these situations, what they are thinking, and what they say. Let your reader have an idea of what your character's intentions are and perhaps even what got them into this situation in the first place.

Giving your character plenty of chances to show up and experience many different situations that they can take action in gives you the opportunity to highlight them from different angles. You can show your reader what that character is like when they're angry, sad, happy, disappointed, unimpressed, hurt, and virtually any other emotion. When you explore your character under these different lights through naturally unfolding events, you make it a lot easier for you to give your reader a more intimate view of your character, too.

Successful stories are those that bring characters to life and make readers believe that they are real people. If you think back to any fiction novel you have read in the past, you can likely conclude that the best ones were the ones where you grieved the end of the book because it felt like you had truly lost someone from your life. *That's* how good your characters can become when you follow these guides and effectively bring them to life for your readers. And, although it may seem difficult, it truly isn't. Follow these steps, and you will have a life-like character playing on the heartstrings of your own readers in no time.

Conclusion

Thank you for reading *"Character Development: Step-by-Step | Essential Story Character Creation, Character Expression and Character Building Tricks Any Writer Can Learn"*.

I hope that you were able to learn plenty of information about how you can create a phenomenal character for your own novel throughout this book. By using the in-depth character creation guide, following the tips on how to build your character, how to make them great, and how to bring them to life, you should have all of the tools you need to make a phenomenal character that will truly draw your readers in and help them generate a sense of emotional attachment to your characters.

The next step is to begin building your characters. If you haven't already, take the time to generate a profile for each of your central characters and all of your biggest minor characters. As well, create modified profiles for your minor characters. Remember that they don't need to be nearly as in-depth, but they do still need to be descriptive enough that you can create a truly strong character. Furthermore, make sure that you pay attention to the tips about how you can make a good character great, and about how you can then bring your characters to life. Ideally, your characters should be brought to life and made so great that your readers feel as though they are friends with that character. They may even grieve the loss of the character when the book ends, and there is nothing left for them to read. Using these tools and tricks, you can certainly create characters that good for your own novel.

Thank you, and best of luck! Have fun writing!

More by Sandy Marsh

Discover all books from the Writing Best Seller Series by Sandy Marsh at:

bit.ly/sandy-marsh

Book 1: *How to Write a Novel*

Book 2: *Outlining*

Book 3: *Story Structure*

Book 4: *Plotting*

Book 5: *Character Development*

Book 6: *How to Write a Screenplay*

Themed book bundles available at discounted prices:

bit.ly/sandy-marsh

www.ingramcontent.com/pod-product-compliance
Lightning Source LLC
Chambersburg PA
CBHW071936150726
47999CB00001B/220